The World Economic Forum

The World Economic Forum is one of the most influential, but least understood, global institutions. Its annual meeting in Davos, Switzerland attracts a significant and powerful audience from the worlds of business, economics, the media and politics. The delegates, who include business and political leaders, as well as NGOs, meet to debate the key issues of global concern and to discuss possible solutions to them. To its critics, however, the Forum is an unaccountable talking shop run by big businesses.

This book explains the history, structure, activities and policies of the World Economic Forum. It takes a balanced approach to its subject, addressing both the positive claims and criticisms of the Forum.

It is a much needed introduction to an important and controversial organization, and will be of considerable interest to students of international relations, international political economy, economics, development and globalization.

Geoffrey Allen Pigman lectures in political economy at Bennington College (Vermont, USA) and is a Visiting Fellow at the Graduate Division of Global Affairs, Rutgers University, Newark. He has lectured in international political economy at the University of Birmingham (UK) and was Director of Graduate Studies of the University of Kent/Brussels School of International Studies, based in Brussels.

Routledge Global Institutions

Edited by Thomas G. Weiss
(CUNY Graduate Center, New York, USA) and
Rorden Wilkinson
(University of Manchester, UK)

The Global Institutions series is designed to provide readers with comprehensive, accessible, and informative guides to the history, structure, and activities of key international organizations. Every volume stands on its own as a thorough and insightful treatment of a particular topic, but the series as a whole contributes to a coherent and complementary portrait of the phenomenon of global institutions at the dawn of the millennium.

Books are written by recognized experts, conform to a similar structure, and cover a range of themes and debates common to the series. These areas of shared concern include the general purpose and rationale for organizations, developments over time, membership, structure, decisionmaking procedures, and key functions. Moreover, current debates are placed in historical perspective alongside informed analysis and critique. Each book also contains an annotated bibliography and guide to electronic information as well as any annexes appropriate to the subject matter at hand.

The volumes currently published or under contract include:

The United Nations and Human Rights (2005)
A Guide for a New Era
by Julie A. Mertus (American University)

The UN Secretary-General and Secretariat (2005)
by Leon Gordenker (Princeton University)

United Nations Global Conferences (2005)
by Michael G. Schechter (Michigan State University)

The UN General Assembly (2005)
by M.J. Peterson (University of Massachusetts, Amherst)

The European Union
by Clive Archer (Manchester Metropolitan University)

The International Labour Organization
by Steve Hughes (University of Newcastle)

The Commonwealth(s) and Global Governance
by Timothy Shaw (Royal Roads University)

The Organization for Security and Co-operation in Europe
by David J. Galbreath (University of Aberdeen)

UNHCR
The Politics and Practice of Refugee Protection into the Twenty-first Century
by Gil Loescher (University of Oxford), James Milner (University of Oxford), and Alexander Betts (University of Oxford)

The World Health Organization
by Kelley Lee (London School of Hygiene and Tropical Medicine)

The World Trade Organization
by Bernard Hoekman (World Bank) and Petros Mavroidis (Columbia University)

The International Organization for Standardization and the Global Economy
Setting Standards
by Craig Murphy (Wellesley College) and JoAnne Yates (Massachusetts Institute of Technology)

The International Olympic Committee
by Jean-Loup Chappelet (IDHEAP Swiss Graduate School of Public Administration) and Btrenda Kübler-Mabbott

For further information regarding the series, please contact:

Craig Fowlie, Publisher, Politics and International Studies
Taylor & Francis
2 Park Square, Milton Park, Abingdon
Oxford OX14 4RN, UK

+44 (0)207 017 6665 Tel.
+44 (0)207 017 6702 Fax

Craig.Fowlie@tandf.co.uk
www.routledge.com

The World Economic Forum

A multi-stakeholder approach to
global governance

Geoffrey Allen Pigman

LONDON AND NEW YORK

First published 2007
by Routledge
2 Park Square, Milton Park, Abingdon, Oxon OX14 4RN

Simultaneously published in the USA and Canada
by Routledge
270 Madison Ave, New York, NY 10016

Routledge is an imprint of the Taylor & Francis Group, an informa business

Transferred to Digital Printing 2008

© 2006 Geoffrey Allen Pigman

Typeset in Times New Roman by
Taylor & Francis Books

British Library Cataloguing in Publication Data
A catalogue record for this book is available from the British Library

Library of Congress Cataloging in Publication Data
A catalog record for this book has been requested

ISBN10: 0-415-70203-8 ISBN13: 978-0-415-70203-4 (hbk)
ISBN10: 0-415-70204-6 ISBN13: 978-0-415-70204-1 (pbk)

Contents

Illustrations

Tables

Figures

Boxes

Foreword

The current volume is the twelfth in a new and dynamic series on "global institutions." The series strives (and, based on the initial volumes we believe, succeeds) to provide readers with definitive guides to the most visible aspects of what we know as "global governance." Remarkable as it may seem, there exist relatively few books that offer in-depth treatments of prominent global bodies and processes, much less an entire series of concise and complementary volumes. Those that do exist are either out of date, inaccessible to the non-specialist reader, or seek to develop a specialized understanding of particular aspects of an institution or process rather than offer an overall account of its functioning. Similarly, existing books have often been written in highly technical language or have been crafted "in-house" and are notoriously self-serving and narrow.

The advent of electronic media has helped by making information, documents, and resolutions of international organizations more widely available, but it has also complicated matters. The growing reliance on the internet and other electronic methods of finding information about key international organizations and processes has served, ironically, to limit the educational materials to which most readers have ready access – namely, books. Public relations documents, raw data, and loosely refereed websites do not make for intelligent analysis. Official publications compete with a vast amount of electronically available information, much of which is suspect because of its ideological or self-promoting slant. Paradoxically, the growing range of purportedly independent websites offering analyses of the activities of particular organizations have emerged, but one inadvertent consequence has been to frustrate access to basic, authoritative, critical, and well researched texts. The market for such has actually been reduced by the ready availability of varying-quality electronic materials.

For those of us who teach, research, and practice in the area, this access to information has been at best frustrating. We were delighted, then, when Routledge saw the value of a series that bucks this trend and provides key reference points to the most significant global institutions. They are betting that serious students and professionals will want serious analyses. We have assembled a first-rate line-up of authors to address that market. Our intention, then, is to provide one-stop shopping for all readers – students (both undergraduate and postgraduate), interested negotiators, diplomats, practitioners from nongovernmental and intergovernmental organizations, and interested parties alike – seeking information about most prominent institutional aspects of global governance.

The World Economic Forum

Few global institutions can claim to have had a significant hand in shaping world politics. The United Nations (UN), the North Atlantic Treaty Organization (NATO), the International Monetary Fund (IMF), the World Bank and World Trade Organization (WTO), and the Group of 7/8 (G7/8) are perhaps the most obvious – and each is the subject of a book in this series. To wield such influence and have a global reach and reputation, each has had to draw upon the political, financial, and/or military resources of its member states. One consequence of this model has been to make these institutions and their executive heads, to greater or lesser degrees, beholden to the wishes of their member states. This, in turn, has ensured that the ability of these institutions to wield influence has been, at best, intermittent. As analysts, we often refer to the staff resources as having the capacity to make independent decisions *on occasion*, but the emphasis is clearly on the relative rarity of such an effort. Moreover, the capacity of these organizations and their secretariats to act autonomously has been continually constrained by anachronistic institutional structures that ensure that they must struggle to retain their relevance in the face of a changing global landscape.

In sharp contrast, the World Economic Forum has consistently influenced both global security *and* economic matters, and it was begun as a private rather than intergovernmental effort. The Forum can claim to have made a difference in the Arab-Israeli peace process and the Uruguay Round of General Agreement on Tariffs and Trade (GATT) negotiations, to name just two prominent examples. What makes the Forum's performance so startling is that it has done so by seemingly little more than facilitating dialogue among political, corporate, academic, and civil society elites. Moreover, the Forum has been able to maintain its relevance through a continual process of reform and regeneration that has kept it at the forefront of world affairs for the past thirty years.

That said, Forum activities have brought not only praise but also a good deal of criticism. Its influence in shaping global economic policy generally, and in facilitating the spread of neoliberal ideas more specifically, has attracted fire from civil society organizations. In terms of process, these populist institutions are concerned about cabals in smoke-filled rooms in luxury hotels in Switzerland gathering to decide the world's fate. In terms of substance, they are concerned about the impact of economic liberalization on, among other things, worker rights, the environment, rural livelihoods, and development in the Global South. Indeed, such was the negative perception of the Forum's impact in some quarters that it spawned a counter-institution in the shape of the World Social Forum (WSF) – a parallel gathering designed to promote social rather than economic development. This "anti-World Economic Forum" has attendees who are rarely part of governmental, intergovernmental, financial, or corporate elites.

Given the World Economic Forum's successes, and its notoriety, it is surprising to note that few serious accounts of the institution exist and that fewer still deal with it in the depth and detail provided here. Given the institution's significance and rule-breaking behavior, there was no question of the need to include a book on the Forum in our series. There was also no question about who we wanted to write the book – Geoffrey Pigman. He has had the kind of access to the Forum that few are able to attain. Not only has he witnessed the Forum in action – a boast only he and the select few that are invited to its events can make. But also he has enjoyed unrivaled access to the Forum's founder and executive chairman, Klaus Schwab, as well as key individuals involved in running Forum events. This insight, in combination with Pigman's literary talent and analytical abilities, has ensured the production of a first-rate book.

We are proud to include this book in our series. It is a must-read, an essential resource for all interested in global governance and world affairs. We heartily recommend it to you and welcome any feedback that you may have.

Thomas G. Weiss, The CUNY Graduate Center, New York, USA
Rorden Wilkinson, University of Manchester, UK
June 2006

Acknowledgements

Many people assisted me in numerous large and small ways as I researched and wrote this book. These acknowledgements are no doubt incomplete – to all those whom I have omitted, please forgive. At the World Economic Forum, I would like to thank Klaus and Hilde Schwab, Ged Davis, Peter Torreele, André Schneider, Rick Samans, and Mark Adams for their thoughts and insights, and all the members of the Forum staff who contributed to the logistics of my visits to the Forum. I would like to thank the editors of Routledge's Global Institutions series, Thomas Weiss and Rorden Wilkinson, for inviting me to undertake this project and providing valued feedback. I would like to thank my academic colleagues Richard Langhorne, Mansour Farhang, Christopher Daase, and Harm Schepel, and the students of the University of Kent's Brussels School of International Studies, especially Kevin Matha, Anthony Deos and John Kotsopoulos, for their enthusiasm for and encouragement of the project. Special thanks go to Kevin Matha for producing the index to this volume. I would like to thank Bennington College for their supportive research culture, without which it would have been much more difficult to complete the book over the past year. And as ever, I thank my mother, Nancy Pigman, for all her love and support over many years.

Abbreviations

CA	Computer Associates
CAFOD	Catholic Agency for Overseas Development
CBI	Confederation of British Industry
CII	Confederation of Indian Industry
CEO	Chief Executive Officer
COO	Chief Operating Officer
CSO	Civil Society Organization
DDR	Doha Development Round
DRN	Disaster Resource Network
EMF	European Management Forum
EU	European Union
FDI	foreign direct investment
GATT	General Agreement on Tariffs and Trade
ICTs	Information and Communications Technologies
IMF	International Monetary Fund
JEI	Jordan Education Initiative
NGO	Non-governmental Organization
MAI	Multilateral Agreement on Investment
MDG	Millennium Development Goals
OECD	Organization for Economic Cooperation and Development
UN	United Nations
WSF	World Social Forum
WTO	World Trade Organization
YGL	Young Global Leaders

Introduction

For one snowy week at the end of each January, over 2,000 people descend upon the chic Swiss ski resort of Davos to think and to talk to each other – to eat, to drink, perhaps to do a bit of skiing and snowboarding, maybe to do a business deal or two – but primarily to think and to talk. Many of these people are famous, or at least well known for being at the top of their respective professions: business, politics and government, international organizations, civil society organizations, charitable foundations, academia, the media, artists, religious institutions. A few snapshots from Davos over the years: US President Bill Clinton talks software interoperability with Microsoft CEO Bill Gates; an Argentine journalist meets global financier George Soros on a ski lift and has a chat; rock star Bono works on Africa poverty eradication with UK Prime Minister Tony Blair; a casual birthday drinks gathering for a policy analyst at the European Commission is "crashed" by retired General and former US Presidential candidate Wesley Clark; film star Sharon Stone "passes the hat" at a panel discussion to raise money to fight malaria in Tanzania.

Originating as a meeting of European businesspeople conceived by a European businessman/academic in 1971 as a vehicle for reclaiming from the Americans a measure of leadership of the international business community, the World Economic Forum has grown over three and a half decades into the premier venue for different types of actors in the global system to discuss the major economic, political and social challenges confronting the world. Its core vision is about bringing together all the different types of major stakeholders in global society to discuss global issues and come up with ways of solving problems. It is a multi-stakeholder vision of global governance – and it is different from anything that came before it.

As a global institution the World Economic Forum is both unique and at its core deeply paradoxical. Whilst sharing important features with other global institutions, it differs from all the others in several key respects. The Forum is fundamentally a knowledge institution: it affects its field of operations by causing the thinking of its members and interlocutors on problems and solutions to change and develop. The Forum's story is a story of the power of words, ideas and discourse. It is an institution that at its heart is all about global governance (itself an as yet largely dark and unexplored landscape), and yet it has no executive or legislative power over a global, or even over any regional or local, domain. But despite having no publicly sanctioned authority as a global actor, the Forum has recorded measurable achievements in the field of contemporary diplomacy. It is a private institution, comprised of a membership of private sector entities, yet through its own efforts it has acquired a public identity and a measure of power and influence in the global public sphere. Although a not-for-profit institution, the Forum functions essentially as a business in its own right, adhering to a strategy of self-financing growth and a deep commitment to building and marketing its brand. And the Forum by its fourth decade came to be a politically contested institution, finding itself on the frontline of the global struggle for the social and political content of globalization. When Managing Director Ged Davis called the Forum a "postmodern" institution, he could not have hit the nail on the head any harder. Understanding the World Economic Forum and its activities is part of a broader project of mapping the topography of contemporary global institutions and emerging instrumentalities of global governance in a post-Westphalian age. The objective of this book is to explore the seeming paradoxes and unique aspects of the Forum, and in doing so to highlight contemporary issues and debates that the Forum narrative illuminates.

In addition to thinking about global problems, the Forum from its inception has thought about itself: what it is, its purposes, what it could be, what it should be. Yet as the Forum expanded its membership and list of participants over its first three decades, others increasingly began to think about the Forum as well. The Forum began to attract more attention not only from policymakers public and private, but from the media, the general public, and in particular from organizations representing interests and positions that the Forum had not made the focus of its debates and brainstorming sessions. By the late 1990s its mission of fostering direct and productive dialogue between Forum members and between members and other invited participants became controversial. Increasingly, outsiders, emboldened by the Forum's own very effective publicity and marketing, contested its complex and seemingly shifting boundaries: between members, invited participants, and those officially excluded altogether, and between the public and private domains into which the information generated by the Forum flows. The controversy drew in sharp relief two competing narratives of the evolution of the World Economic Forum and its role in changing global society.[1] The first narrative is arguably symbolized by the Shar-pei, a cuddly puppy, homely but lovable, born baggy with folds of surplus skin and fur into which s/he grows steadily into a finely proportioned purebred adult dog. In this tale, the Forum can be understood as an organization conceived ahead of its time, an embryonic stoa for global problem solving created at the beginning of the contemporary, information-age global economy. The Forum's structure and *esprit de corps* rendered it able to expand its membership, scope of issues covered, and range of participants, to grow from a European to a global focus and to stay at the ever faster advancing leading edge of information technology transformation. In the Shar-pei story, the Forum has also been able to grow into the globalization discourse as it has emerged and evolved by embracing a steadily wider range of participants and ideas, which in turn has made the Forum's core corporate membership better informed and has constructed member firms' perceptions of their interests in the direction of "entrepreneurship in the global public interest."

A wolf in sheep's clothing is emblematic of the second narrative, which was embraced by many of the Forum's critics (see Chapter 6 on "existential" vs. "instrumental" critics). This account portrays the Forum as a cabal of wealthy elites in business and government that has been meeting for several decades to facilitate an agenda of integration of the global economy intended to benefit large transnational firms and governments of industrialized nation-states at the expense of consumers, the environment, the poor, and local or non-global culture. The discussions serve as venues in which ideas and policies designed to benefit large firms and governments are legitimated and consecrated. In this narrative the Forum started small, not eliciting criticism, but then took advantage of information technology to grow to dominate the discourse of globalization, becoming a nodal point for servants of global capital against local, agricultural, environmental and social-cultural interests. For adherents of this view, the Forum's public information face serves as a cover or price of legitimacy for its core function as a private venue for its members and invited guests, including political leaders, to exchange information and make business deals.

Examining the record of the Forum's evolution one could probably find enough supporting information to sustain both narratives plausibly, depending on one's own political and ideological presuppositions and leanings. But focusing on the narratives alone begs a series of basic questions that the two narratives would tend to answer differently. What is the significance of the structure of the Forum as a membership organization? What is its agenda and purpose? Whose interests does it favour? What is the relationship of the Forum to the dominant discourse of globalization? How has the organization changed and adapted, and in response to which principal factors? To what extent, if at all, the competing narratives of the Forum's evolution are useful in terms of understanding the Forum and its relationship to discourses of globalization, will become evident through the course of the analysis that follows and will be revisited in the concluding chapter.

The investigation also generates a potentially more interesting finding. The version of technology-driven, market-liberalizing globalization that the Forum was effectively promoting on behalf of its members in the 1990s, notwithstanding the Forum's longstanding commitment to building global public goods, appears to have triggered an unintended process whereby the World Economic Forum itself changed in such a way as to make it more likely to be able to achieve its social as well as economic objectives. Proponents and opponents of the liberal market version of globalization promoted by the Forum alike can agree that liberalization favours some interests and disadvantages others. One may agree or disagree with the liberal public choice axiom that undertaking liberalization will always net more social gain than imposing the costs of liberalization upon the whole economy, even after the losers are compensated with sidepayments paid for from the gains from liberalization (worker retraining, investment in environmental protection, funding for local culture, etc.). But the problem remains that it is difficult politically in a democratic system to legislate the sidepayments required to spread the gains from liberalization fully amongst all sectors of society, or at least sufficiently enough to maintain ongoing popular support for liberalization.[2] Hence the market-liberalizing version of globalization is bound to be contested by an ever more vocal band of critics. Yet political constituencies favouring socially embedded markets can be strengthened through the social reconstruction of interests perceived by firms and other stakeholders that can occur through repeated discursive interactions between different types of stakeholders in the global economy at venues like Davos. One significant effect of the advance in communications technology upon the discourse of globalization was to shift the content of the discussions at Davos and other Forum summits and to broaden the range of participants to include an increased number of civil society organizations and other representatives of a broader spectrum of civil society than had participated in the Forum's early years. This change raises the prospect that building the nation-state level and cross-border political coalitions needed to make the sidepayments required to spread the benefits of market-liberalizing globalization may become easier, an objective very much consonant with the Forum's broad goals, even if through a causality not envisioned or planned by Forum managers or members.[3] The story of this transformation is one of the plotlines that unfold in this book.

Just as the Forum by its nature is resistant to capture by any grand narrative, so too must be the narratives of the Forum as told in this book. Within this text are many paths to familiarity with the Forum: straight description of histories and institutional structures, analysis of discourses and images, and subjective accounts of how participants interact through the Forum. Numerous linkages that are surprising and unanticipated emerge. For example, the narrative of the Forum's evolution is inextricably entangled with the narrative of India's emergence as an economic powerhouse, for reasons that will become evident as the story unfolds. To develop an understanding of this sort of institution, multiple, methodologically diverse and overlapping accounts are required. With this in mind, the chapters of the book are organized as follows. The first two chapters give overviews of the history and the institutional structure of the Forum. The third chapter places the activities of the Forum in greater theoretical context, relating them to contemporary academic debates over topics such as identity and diplomacy. The second half of the book looks at contemporary activities of the Forum and the questions that they raise in greater detail. Chapter 4 looks closely at two major Forum meetings in 2005, the Annual Meeting at Davos and the India Economic Summit in New Delhi, using two different methods to analyze narratives of each meeting. The fifth chapter examines the knowledge output of the Forum, discussing how the Forum constructs discourse, how it uses information technology, the content of the Forum's research, and the Initiatives, the public-private partnerships that the Forum is organizing to implement solutions for global problems. Chapter 6 discusses critics and criticisms of the Forum and examines how the Forum has been engaging with its critics. The final chapter considers the main questions that the Forum faces going forward: how the Forum needs to change and the global issues that it needs to be ready to address in the future.

1 A multi-stakeholder approach

An historical overview

Founding of the Forum: a European resurgence

The World Economic Forum was conceived in Europe in 1971, a time when the international monetary system of gold parities and fixed exchange rates established at Bretton Woods in 1944 was collapsing and European governments were challenging the postwar economic dominance of the United States. Servan-Schreiber's well known Gaullist tract *Le défi americain* (translated into English as *The American Challenge*) articulated growing European fears that US firms were buying up European industry.[1] It was also a time when European firms were challenging the paternalistic model of relations between governments and businesses that had prevailed since World War II, at least in Western Europe.[2] The evolution of technology to facilitate movements of goods, services and capital was accelerating, as evidenced by the growth in international trade and the rapid rise in the late 1960s of offshore currency balances ("Eurodollars") and cross-border direct investment. With the explicit backing of French Gaullists and other nationalist politicians, European firms were ready to take on their American-based counterparts, which had expanded their global market activity dramatically in the two decades following World War II.

Yet 1971 was early in the development of the various phenomena and processes of economic, political and social convergence and inter-penetration across territorial boundaries that have subsequently come to be tagged by the media and scholars as "globalization." Cox characterizes the period in which the Forum was founded as a turning point in the development of capitalism from an international to a global economy.[3] The post-World War II, Bretton Woods system, wherein nation-state governments generally exercised control over their domestic economies and regulated their interaction with the rest of the world economy, was being supplanted by a phase in which nation-state governments took on the often reduced role of adjusting their own economies to change in a global economy less subservient to national or multilateral regulation. Globalization, however, not only refers to phenomena and processes, but to a discourse that is social-cultural in character and is composed of information flows, debate, representations of interests and exercises of power by forces able to do so in behalf of their interests.[4] The particular discourse of globalization that has emerged has had proponents and opponents since well before it was identified and debated as such by academia and, more recently, by the rest of global civil society (i.e. the aggregation of global and local social forces outside of formal organs of governance). One of the most significant functions of the World Economic Forum has been to serve as a principal venue for debating issues in this predominantly neoliberal, and until recently dominant, globalization discourse. Hence it is important to recognize that the Forum began its operations at the time when that discourse began to attract participants and interest, and its importance grew as its main stock in trade, information, came to be demanded ever increasingly by members and non-members alike. This timing enables holders of the Shar-pei view to see the Forum as essentially an organization that emerged just before its time, or right at the beginning of its time, and that was able to grow rapidly as demand for its information output grew.

The story that the Forum tells of its own evolution is one of a private sector nonprofit foundation born of a meeting of European captains of industry under the patronage of the European Commission and European industrial associations. The story of the Forum's creation and subsequent development up to the present day is also closely intertwined with that of its founder and leader for three and a half decades, Klaus Schwab. After chairing a meeting of European business leaders in January 1971 in Davos, Switzerland, to "discuss a coherent strategy for European business to face challenges in the international marketplace," Schwab, then a professor of business policy at the University of Geneva, founded the European Management Forum to institutionalize an annual summit of European business leaders at Davos. Born in Ravensburg, Germany, in 1938 to a family of Swiss descent, as a child Schwab's family lived close to the German-Swiss border and were able to cross the border freely throughout World War II. Struck by the artificiality of a territorial boundary between war and peace, Schwab recognized early the importance of dialogue and reconciliation to conflict resolution.[5] As a young man in postwar Western Europe, Schwab put this into practice by chairing a French-German youth movement in Baden-Wurttemberg. Schwab obtained two Ph.D.s, in mechanical engineering from the Federal Institute of Technology (Zurich), and in economics from the University of Fribourg. In the course of his studies for the engineering degree he spent a year working in a factory, to which he attributes his understanding of and respect for labor unions.[6] Schwab made a name for himself in management in the 1960s by applying Harvard management techniques to the implementation of mergers between European firms. Employed by Swiss industrial group Escher Wyss in 1967, he managed successfully the group's merger with Sulzer Group, a significant challenge for a young executive, but one that still did not challenge Klaus Schwab sufficiently as he looked forward. Appointed to a part-time professorship at the Centre des Etudes Industrielles in Geneva in 1969, Schwab found that he also felt "not completely challenged" at the university and sought to build a greater role for himself and his talents in the wider world.

Having registered for a study year at the Harvard University Kennedy School of Government's Littauer Center in 1966–7 had enabled Klaus Schwab to take second-year courses at the Harvard Business School, an opportunity not customarily permitted to non-MBA students and one which gave him a deeper appreciation of contemporary American management approaches and techniques. Schwab's year at Harvard served as a catalyst for his idea to establish the European Management Forum as a vehicle to bring these approaches and techniques to European firms. He befriended the Dean of Harvard Business School, George P. Baker, who was impressed by Schwab's ingenuity at figuring out how to take Business School courses without being in the MBA program. Schwab subsequently asked Baker to chair the first meeting of the EMF. Whilst at Harvard Schwab had the opportunity to meet Henry Kissinger, Robert Reischauer, John Kenneth Galbraith and other leading US academics, and through their conversations developed an interest in global issues, and in particular the relationship between security and the business climate. Schwab conceived of the European Management Forum as an opportunity for new kinds of conversations to take place between senior managers of European firms, in which a range of regional and global business, economic, political and social issues that affected the European business community could be addressed.

From the start he envisioned the Forum as involving close cooperation between European business and political leaders, so he wrote to Jean Rey, President of the European Commission, to seek the Commission's advice, support and participation. Rey suggested two commissioners to serve as interlocutors for the Forum, Raymond Barre and Altiero Spinelli. Rey promised Commission support for the Forum under two conditions: one, that the Forum be established as a not-for-profit institution, and two, that it hold its meetings on European Community territory. Both conditions were agreed, as Schwab had planned the Forum to operate on a not-for-profit basis, and at that time Rey and Schwab expected Switzerland, the intended location of the Forum, to join the European Community shortly thereafter.

The stakeholder theory: from management to global society

The first European Management Forum meeting was held in Davos in January 1971, with Harvard economist John Kenneth Galbraith and Rand Corporation military strategist and futurist Herman Kahn serving as keynote speakers.[7] Modest in size to start compared to the annual meetings of recent years, the meeting was attended by 444 participants from a wide range of West European firms. From its inception the Davos Annual Meeting reflected Klaus Schwab's interest in communications technology, featuring then-futuristic closed circuit television, enabling participants to watch conference speakers from outside of the halls.[8] The initial three annual Davos meetings concentrated on how European firms could catch up with US management methods. One of Schwab's primary objectives was to encourage European managers to adopt the "stakeholder" approach to management. Schwab had developed a stakeholder theory of management of industrial manufacturing firms in the 1960s and co-wrote a text, *Moderne Unternehmenführung im Maschinenbau*.[9] In the book, Schwab argued that, in order to be effective in maximizing a firm's potential, managers need to take account of the interests of all the stakeholders in the firm: not only shareholders but customers and clients, employees, managerial staff, and the broader interests of the communities within which the firm is situated, including neighbors in the immediate proximity of the firm, governments, and fellow users of the environment in which the firm operates. The stakeholder approach contrasts sharply with other, more classical approaches to management, such as more narrow profit-and-loss accounting or the East Asian approach focusing on dominating market share. Schwab envisioned that managers of European firms, by adopting the stakeholder approach, could raise their game competitively in response to the challenge posed by their more efficient American challengers.[10] The stakeholder model of corporate management, Schwab found, lent itself naturally to governance in a broader sense. Solving problems – whether they lay within a firm, a civil society organization (CSO), a nation-state, a region, or were global – could be done most effectively by taking account of the interests of all the stakeholders in the relevant issue or problem, and by encouraging all the stakeholders to participate in the problem solving process. The challenge of the multi-stakeholder approach to governance and problem solving lay in that different stakeholders are different types of groups or entities, which do not represent themselves and communicate to other bodies in the same way. A mid-sized enterprise, a trade union, an environmental activist group, a county government, a university and a business association, are each very different sorts of entities, but they may all have a stake in a particular issue or situation specific to their location or focus. Hence there are times when they need to talk to and listen to one another if they are to be able to address serious issues that can affect them all. Klaus Schwab's project (see Figure 1.1) was to devise a venue to make that type of communication not just possible, but productive and fruitful.

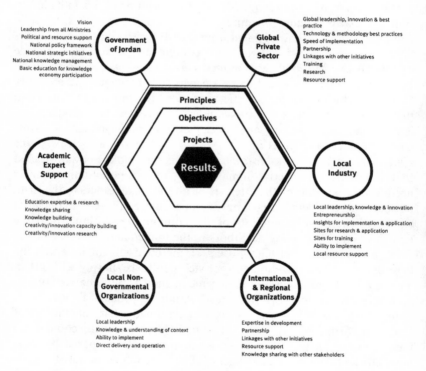

Figure 1.1 Klaus Schwab's multi-stakeholder theory of governance, as later adapted and diagrammed in the Forum's Jordan Education Initiative promotional literature.

Milestones of evolution

Klaus Schwab recounts the story of how his vision of what would become the World Economic Forum evolved as one of "milestones." According to Schwab, his vision of how the European Management Forum would develop was not a master template that he had in mind from the start. As they went along, Schwab and the Forum's managers adjusted the focus of their topics for discussion in response to the Forum's members and, crucially, in response to global events. Schwab cites the first major milestone to affect the Forum's evolution as the major global political and economic events of 1973: the final collapse of the Bretton Woods fixed exchange rate system and the Arab-Israeli War and resultant OPEC oil boycott of Western industrial countries.[11] The Forum identifies the fall 1973 oil crisis as the catalyst for expanding its focus from management issues to political, economic and social issues: major strategic factors in the global environment that firms needed to monitor.[12] At this point the Forum took the decision to invite political leaders to participate directly in the discussions of the January 1974 Davos meeting. The organization also decided to hold Country Forums as venues for international business leaders to meet with political, economic and trades union leaders of individual countries, with the first meetings taking place in Brussels and Paris in 1973. By 1975 fourteen country meetings were held; the process was extended to developing countries in 1977 and to the People's Republic of China in 1979. Country Forums later evolved into the regional agenda and summits of the current period.

Quick to appreciate the significance of the Chinese Communist Party Congress' liberalization of China's economic policy, Schwab invited the Chinese government to send representatives to the 1979 Davos Annual Meeting. The Chinese delegates' attendance made the Forum the first international CSO to engage with China. Schwab visited China in April 1979, speaking on the multi-stakeholder model of governance. The first China country meeting, a symposium for Chinese and foreign business leaders, took place in Beijing in June 1980.[13] Today known as the China Business Summit, the long running annual meeting is co-sponsored by the Forum and the China Enterprise Confederation, a leading Chinese business association founded in 1979 in conjunction with China's economic liberalization. On its website in 2000, the Forum claimed to have brought more businesses to China than any other organization, and to having "had a substantial impact on the economic reform policies of China."[14]

The next milestone that Schwab cites is 1976, the year in which the Forum began its shift from a primarily European toward a global focus. The EMF undertook a major project to improve business relations between Europe and the Middle East. They invited twenty Middle Eastern and twenty Western banks to underwrite a symposium for Arab business leaders, which was held at Montreux, Switzerland. One thousand Arab business leaders and 1,000 European business leaders attended the symposium, which had the objective of improving relationships that had been strained severely by the 1973 oil embargo. The symposium had the effect of structuring the future relationship between the European Community and the Gulf Cooperation Council, the then recently founded regional economic cooperation organization for states bounding the Persian Gulf. Following up on a successful symposium, the Forum replicated the process the following year with a Europe-Latin America symposium, a second Europe-Arab symposium in 1978 and a second Europe-Latin America symposium in 1979.[15] Over time this interregional approach to improving business relations evolved into a more focused approach of holding national meetings in countries such as Brazil, Argentina, Malaysia and others, with the number of annual national symposia held gradually climbing to 15–20 per year, as they too became part of the Forum's regional agenda.

The year 1976 also marked a major structural evolution for the Forum: the EMF Foundation transformed itself into a membership organization, with membership limited in principle to "the 1,000 foremost global enterprises," ranked by a combination of rank within industry/country, extent of their global activity, leadership in their industry/region, corporate health and reputation (see Chapter 2 for further details on membership).[16] At that time Schwab and other board members began recruiting top business executives from the United States to attend Davos, with IBM chairman Thomas Watson and Pepsi Cola CEO Don Kendall among the first to attend.[17] A further major milestone occurred in 1979, when the Forum began publishing research, a key step toward the realization of Schwab's objective of transforming the Forum from being primarily about organizing conferences into a organization that leverages fully its knowledge-generating capacities. Beginning by producing an annual World Competitiveness Report that assesses the relative competitiveness of the business climate in a small group of countries for the benefit of its members, the Forum has steadily expanded the scope of its annual research output to include other industry- and region-specific competitiveness reports, an annual magazine and, more recently, concise strategic insight reviews of key topics for global leaders. The Forum has also diversified into major specific research projects under the auspices of Forum Initiatives (see Chapter 5).

Growing and going global: the 1980s

The 1980s saw the Forum expand its activities in several significant directions. In order to secure the position of the Davos annual meeting as a "must attend" event for top business leaders, assuring the regular participation of top-level representatives of other stakeholders in the global economy, would be essential. In order to achieve this the Forum staff realized that they had to do more to convince senior political and economic leaders of the value of participating in Davos. Beginning in 1982 the Forum invited cabinet-level government officials and leaders of multilateral organizations such as the World Bank, International Monetary Fund (IMF), and the General Agreement on Tariffs and Trade (GATT), to meet together with one another in an informal gathering concurrent with the annual Davos meeting, in addition to participating in the Davos meeting itself. The Forum was organizing a new setting for informal communication between political and economic leaders, in which they could get to know one another, exchange ideas and work on ongoing issues and problems without having to produce a communiqué, treaty or other finished product. The Informal Gathering of World Economic Leaders, as it became known, was sufficiently well received that it sparked a steady increase in the number, and relative importance, of political and economic leaders attending. Amongst the early fruits of these informal meetings of this group of stakeholders, the Forum counts a meeting of trade ministers in Lausanne in 1982 that led to the launching of the GATT Uruguay Round in 1986.[18]

Beginning in 1983, the Forum repeated this successful format by hosting informal gatherings at Davos for international media leaders, nongovernmental economic research organizations, and regional and municipal government officials. In the same year at Davos the Forum began hosting meetings of CEOs of major firms by industrial sector using the informal gathering format. These Industry Governors' Meetings, as they became known, began in 1983 with a gathering of CEOs of the global information technology sector, but by 1995 gatherings had been held for ten different industrial sectors. The meetings serve several purposes: they allow CEOs based in different parts of the world to meet regularly, itself a difficult logistical task; to get to know one another informally away from a media-charged climate of speculation about mergers, acquisitions or other deals; and to develop a sense of the global role of their industry and how it relates to the broader global community. Hence the sectoral gatherings facilitate cooperation between firms and other stakeholders that advance global public and social purposes as well as the consummation of private business deals.[19]

The Forum's geographical reach expanded again in 1985 as it followed up its opening to China with a move into India, a huge country with a potential market of already nearly 1 billion people at the time, but one that had experienced slow growth under economic policies that had favoured import-substituting industrialization since independence. Once again early to become sensitive to the significance of market-opening in developing countries that would become major global economic players, Schwab responded quickly to Prime Minister Rajiv Gandhi's intensification of economic reforms that had recently begun on a more limited basis under the premiership of Indira Gandhi, seeing a role for the Forum. When Rajiv Gandhi visited Geneva in 1984, Colette Mathur, now the Forum's Director for South Asia, approached him about establishing an annual country meeting in India. In 1985 the Forum's first India Economic Summit was held in New Delhi, in conjunction with four major Indian business associations. The following year the Forum formed a partnership with the Confederation of Indian Industry (CII), one of the leading associations of Indian businesses, to co-sponsor the annual India meetings, establishing a relationship that has grown significantly over twenty years in tandem with the growth of the Forum, the CII and the liberalizing Indian economy.[20] The Forum and the CII together have provided the venue and the context for much of the debate between government officials, businesses and civil society organizations over the course of Indian economic liberalization. The Forum-CII partnership has proved to be one of the most enduring and significant cooperative relationships in the Forum's history to date, and it has enabled the Forum to claim a degree of credit for India's extraordinary growth over the past two decades. (See Chapter 5 for a more in-depth discussion of the 2005 India Economic Summit.)

Acknowledging and embracing the increasingly global nature of its membership and purview, the Foundation changed its name in 1987 from the European Management Forum to the World Economic Forum. In keeping with the more global title, the Forum began the first of a series of high-level initiatives to resolve intergovernmental diplomatic conflicts extending beyond Europe, by bringing interlocutors together, either at the annual Davos meeting or elsewhere under the Forum's auspices. As the Cold War ended, the pace of intergovernmental diplomacy around the globe accelerated dramatically, and the World Economic Forum was at or near the center of the openings of dialogue, offering a venue and acting as a facilitator when required. At the 1987 Davos meeting, then West German Foreign Minister Hans-Dietrich Genscher called upon summit attendees to "give Gorbachev a chance," encouraging a spirit of East-West cooperation across the public and private sectors that built support for ending the Cold War. At Davos in January 1988, prime ministers Andreas Papandreou of Greece and Turgut Ozal of Turkey held their first substantive talks and subsequently signed the Davos Declaration, an agreement to reduce heightened tensions that had threatened war between the two NATO member states.[21] In January 1989, officials of the North Korean and South Korean government held their first ministerial-level discussions at Davos, and at the same time West German Chancellor Helmut Kohl and East German Prime Minister Hans Modrow met to discuss German reunification. In 1990 Mexican President Carlos Salinas de Gortari initiated conversations at Davos that led to the negotiation of the North American Free Trade Agreement (NAFTA).[22] South African President F. W. de Klerk held his first meeting with Nelson Mandela and Zulu Chief Mangosuthu Buthelezi outside of South Africa at Davos in 1992, and at the 1994 Davos meeting Israeli Foreign Minister Shimon Peres and Palestine Liberation Organization Chairman Yasser Arafat signed a draft agreement on Gaza and Jericho as part of the Oslo peace process.[23]

The breaking down of barriers between East and West in Europe at the end of the 1980s occasioned an ambitious, if technically unsuccessful, expansion in the technological platform for communication between the Forum's members and constituents. From the Forum's inception, Schwab had placed a high priority on the adoption of the latest technologies to facilitate and promote communication and interaction through the Forum. In the late 1980s Schwab saw an opportunity to be an early adopter of the next generation in communications technology: a broadband intranet for members and constituents that would offer secure, private videoconferencing, discussion groups, Forum documentation and information, and email facilities.[24] In the year of the fall of the Berlin Wall, 1989, the Forum announced the launch of WELCOM, which the Foundation describes as "the first electronic networking system between the Foundation's members and constituents."[25] On their website in 2000 the Forum characterized the project accurately as "pioneering" and indicated that it was the basis for a "strong digital information and communications dimension" for its subsequent activities.

Although the Forum invested a considerable amount of funds and effort in WELCOM over nine years, the platform ultimately did not succeed, largely because it depended upon communications hardware and internet technology that was not yet sufficiently robust to deliver the degree of reliable broadband service required. And as with most new communications technologies, in advance of becoming fully operational it was open to question whether Forum members would make full use of WELCOM.[26] But although it was unsuccessful, WELCOM paved the way for the initiation of a subsequent generation broadband internal two-way video communications and email network in 1997 that serves Davos attendees in their rooms and meeting places.[27] Today attendees at Davos carry "Davos Communicator" iPaq personal communication devices, through which they can read the program, book places at panel sessions, download supporting information and communicate with other participants.

"Going public": the 1990s and 2000s

This upgrade of the infrastructure for communication between Forum members prefaced a series of new meetings and initiatives to address the changing post-Cold War politico-economic climate in the 1990s. The first post-Cold War decade would be characterized by intensified communications, using a growing range of channels, between a now larger and more integrated family of stakeholders in the global economy. As former socialist states became "economies in transition," and developing countries restructured their economies to meet heightened global competitive demands, new firms, business associations, international institutions and civil society organizations emerged. The Forum geared up in response to help governments, firms and CSOs in transition and developing states communicate with one another and with existing stakeholders in the global economy. The Forum held a pan-European summit of heads of state and government in 1990 to "re-introduce West and East European leaders to one another after the Cold War."[28] Stepping up their programme of regional summits, The Forum instituted an annual Europe-East Asia economic summit beginning in 1992, a Southern Africa economic summit beginning in 1993, a Middle East-North Africa summit from 1994, a Mercosur summit from 1995, and a Central and Eastern European summit from 1996. The Forum created new knowledge networks for different groups, including young politicians, business leaders, academics, arts and media figures, (initially known as "Global Leaders for Tomorrow," later "Young Global Leaders"), cultural and arts leaders ("World Arts

Forum"), and business and academic leaders in high-technology sectors (industry summits for "Global Growth Companies"). In 1998 the Forum launched the Business Consultative Council, a venue at the annual Davos summit for heads of business associations and United Nations organizations to meet and develop closer permanent relations. As good governance came to be seen as a core enabling component for economic development in both developing countries and economies in transition alike, the Forum in 2003 launched its Global Governance Initiative, to serve as an independent monitor of global progress towards the 2015 deadline for achieving the United Nations' Millennium Development Goals.

The expanding size and scope of the organization and its activities in the early 1990s posed questions of internal structure that the Forum by its own admission was forced to address. Since becoming a membership organization in 1976, the Forum had a core membership of the world's leading transnational firms that paid the Foundation's costs by subscription, and for whom the Forum's highest level of benefits was intended. By 1993 that core membership reached 1,000 firms. Arrayed around the core membership were governments, other institutions and individuals, variously described by the Forum as "constituents," "participants" and "communities," whose participation in Forum activities was by invitation of the Foundation itself on the basis that they either were target beneficiaries of Forum objectives or else were in a position to contribute to those objectives and interests. In the early 1990s Forum members had a range of concerns about how the Davos annual meeting had evolved: some felt it had become too large; some thought the shift in focus toward global political and policy issues had gone too far at the expense of issues with a specifically business focus; some felt the content of the seminars at the Davos meetings was inadequate.[29] In 1993 the Forum decided to reassert control over participation in its activities by ending the possibility for firms that were not members of the Forum to attend the Davos meeting by paying a fee: "In order to reinforce the club character of its networks, the Foundation limits its activities to members and to their special guests only."[30] Yet in that same time frame they experimented with new channels for participation, in 1993 creating 300 Forum Fellows, experts across a range of fields to advise the Forum and contribute to its activities. In 1994 they instituted two new categories of membership, one for "Global Growth Companies" that were fast-growing and entrepreneurial, and another for firms with a more regional than global focus.

By the runup to the 2000 Davos meeting, the World Economic Forum by one account was in an enviable position. It had become a household name amongst the world's educated public, with a dedicated Special Report section prominently displayed and permanently located on the *Financial Times*' website, FT.com, that in turn linked the public by one click of a mouse to the Forum's own website. The Foundation was managing with care to continue to enlarge the membership and range of participants, increasing popular awareness of the Forum and its mission as well as access to its research output, whilst at the same time maintaining the elite cachet attached to attendance at Davos itself. The summit's ever more star-studded guest list, topped in 1999 by US Vice President and leading presidential candidate Al Gore,[31] was to be crowned in 2000 by Bill Gates, then CEO of the largest company in the world by market capitalization at the time, Microsoft (and in the process of becoming one of the world's leading philanthropists), and Bill Clinton, president of the wealthiest country in the world by national output, the United States.

Yet by the late 1990s the very visible success of the Forum, which the organization publicized and in effect championed so effectively, attracted critics who did not share all of the same visions of globalization as the Foundation and its member firms. Concurrently a shift in perceptions of the global economy and the role of big business was underway, as the post-Cold War, dot.com boom gave way to the dot.crash and the "Kleptogate" financial and accounting scandals that affected a series of large firms like Enron and WorldCom. The neoliberal, corporate-driven version of globalization came under challenge from a widening segment of global civil society, and the World Economic Forum had made itself a highly visible face of the sort of globalization that drove the 1990s. A wide range of CSOs and other political and social groupings with different visions of what the global economy could be and should be petitioned to attend the Davos meeting and take an active part in the discussions. Others still threatened to come to Davos uninvited to protest the proceedings. The Davos 2000 summit was disrupted by protesters, some of whom were able to evade the efforts of security personnel to keep them from reaching the resort village by skiing in. Protesting groups staged demonstrations in front of the Centre des Congrès where the majority of the meetings take place, and, in a move intended to capture maximum media attention and symbolic power, trashed the local McDonald's in Davos.

Recognizing that this coalition of civil society organizations, which was similar to that which had disrupted the December 1999 World Trade Organization ministerial meeting in Seattle with violent protests, was intent on making its presence felt at Davos, the Forum responded by inviting a limited number of organizations to attend the summit and participate in "peripheral" dialogues, thereby granting them a degree of participation that would serve to co-opt massive protest whilst not changing the core of planned and structured events and their respective participants. Some CSO representatives wishing to participate viewed the opportunities granted by the Forum as insufficient.[32] Yet because the Forum is not a deliberative or legislative body, and the Davos meeting not a summit of the sort in which political or business leaders undertake to reach agreement on a specific act or issue, the inclusion of additional actors with different objectives and agendas is significant. If by the Forum's own measure its output is increased knowledge and changed understandings of global social and economic issues for its members and participants, then the inclusion of the protest groups changed the output of Davos. Major political leaders attending the Annual Meeting, including President Clinton and UK Prime Minister Tony Blair, and the leaders of the major global firms, such as Bill Gates, were obliged to engage publicly with the alternative agendas of the CSOs.[33] (See Chapter 6 for more information on how the Forum has engaged with its critics.)

The 11 September 2001 al-Qa'eda attacks combined with the dot.crash and Kleptogate scandals further to challenge perceptions of the inevitability of globalization and global economic growth, and the World Economic Forum was swift to respond. The Forum began a new chapter in January 2002 by moving the Annual Meeting from its traditional Davos venue to a setting that could hardly be more different from the cozy and private atmosphere of the Swiss Alps: New York City. Announced as a move intended to show solidarity with the beleaguered city in the aftermath of the 11 September attacks, the Forum's decision to shift the summit venue was based in part upon Schwab's fears that many US participants would be reluctant to make their usual trip to Davos in light of the post-9/11 security environment and the recession that the attacks had accentuated.[34] The move to New York also played a role in negotiations underway between the Forum and the Swiss government over security arrangements and costs of holding the summit in Davos. Following the 2001 protests at Davos, both Forum management and Swiss officials recognized the need for greater security measures, but Swiss authorities concerned about the added costs sought to work out a mutually agreeable formula with officials of the Forum.[35] The economics of holding the annual meeting in New York with its 4,000 attendees and support staff were widely debated in advance of the Forum's arrival at the Waldorf-Astoria Hotel, chosen to be the Forum's Manhattan headquarters. Advance estimates provided by the quasi-governmental tourism promotion body NYC & Company of direct revenue to be generated for New York by the Forum, figuring a typical visitor's likely spend on food, shopping, transport and lodging, ranged from $13 million up to $19.4 million, reaching the higher figure if a standard multiplier of 1.5 to estimate ripple effects of tourist spending on the local economy was factored in. By contrast, the cost to the city of providing the required security to protect the Forum participants and New Yorkers was estimated at over $11 million.[36] Cristyne Nicholas, President of NYC & Company, called the Forum's presence in New York "priceless" in terms of its ability to communicate to the rest of the world that post-9/11 New York was again "open for business."[37]

Staging the Annual Meeting in the heart of the world's leading financial center and the most densely developed city on earth invited a degree of human interface between the members of the World Economic Forum, its other invited participants, and the rest of global civil society that had never occurred before. Among New Yorkers still recovering from the physical, economic and emotional effects of the al-Qa'eda attacks four months earlier, anxiety was heightened over potential risks from externally organized violence against the Forum, and about possible disruption to their daily lives caused by the Annual Meeting activities: organized protests and police restrictions to protect Forum participants from the protests. Many businesses gave their employees detailed instructions as to how to protect themselves and minimize their exposure to potential threats. In a confidential security memo to New York-based staff, one global financial services firm advised: "To the extent that you can, avoid going near protests." The same memo concluded, "At this time, the authorities anticipate a relatively peaceful event. Hopefully that will mean business as usual for us."[38]

In the event, fears of a disruptive clash between the Forum and civil society were misplaced. Forum members and their invited guests descended upon New York and made extensive use of the wide range of venues that the city offers for entertaining celebrities. From an Elton John performance at a party at the Four Seasons, to a dinner hosted by Gregory Carr and Peter Gabriel for the human rights CSO Witness, to the annual Steve and Robert Forbes-hosted "Friday Nightcap" party held on this occasion at the 21 Club and attended by Bill Clinton and Hamid Karzai, New York's restaurants, bars, clubs and hotels put on their best shows for their global guests.[39] The civil society protests, the first demonstrations to be permitted in the city since 9/11, were overwhelmingly peaceful and drew large crowds of participants and onlookers despite extraordinarily high levels of security. The main event, a march down Madison Avenue and past the Waldorf-Astoria hotel, organized by the alter-globalization umbrella organization Another World is Possible, created a dramatic visual contrast of marchers in colorful costumes, dancing, singing, operating giant puppets and Chinese New Year-style dragons, all hemmed in by miles of metal security barricades and platoons of mounted police and riot-equipped officers on foot. Thousands of New Yorkers lined the streets to take in the spectacle and, in a sense, to reclaim a part of civic life that had been interrupted so suddenly by the destruction of the Twin Towers.

Forum management realized that the Davos-in-New York venue for the 2002 Annual Meeting was a leap in the dark. Schwab and the Forum's senior managers have never been afraid to experiment, even if not all the experiments are successful. According to the Forum spokesperson Charles McLean, the unanswered question prior to the event was: "will the spirit of Davos travel?"[40] After the event opinion was still divided. The meeting was criticized widely for a variety of reasons, principally because the unique atmosphere of Davos, which gathers the participants into a "closed universe" in which activities are limited largely to talking or skiing, was lost to the teeming bustle of Manhattan. The New York setting also could not solve the problem of the steadily expanding list of summit attendees, both Forum members and other invited participants, which was making the sort of chance encounters and intimate conversations that had made the invitation to Davos so sought-after progressively less likely. Yet bringing the Forum's Annual Meeting to New York was an important success for a number of reasons. Most New Yorkers were pleased with the visit of the Forum to their city: a reasonable amount of business was generated for a city still struggling to recover from the impact of the 2001 attacks; there was neither disruptive violence or unduly onerous interruption to the rhythm of daily life for ordinary citizens; and New Yorkers were able to demonstrate to the world graphically that their city continued to be a place where the world's important people and businesses want to be.

The period since 2002 has seen the Forum's research Initiatives (see Chapter 5) grow substantially in number and importance, ranging from development of a business network to provide relief for natural disasters to a major joint venture with the Jordanian government to improve the quality of education for Jordanian children. The growth and success of the Initiatives have brought the Forum closer to realizing Klaus Schwab's vision of transcending the persisting public perception of the Forum as predominantly a conference organizer and becoming a generator and enabler of global public policy. After the Forum reached an agreement on costs and provision of security with Swiss authorities, in 2003 the annual meeting returned to Davos. The size and space problem remained serious, by some accounts. Yet the capacity participation at Davos 2005 indicates that size, which is perhaps the Forum's main problem, remains an indicator of strength: the desirability of an invitation to Davos, for those "A-list" participants most sought after by other attendees as well as for others, endures. Why this is so is explored in the chapters that follow. The next chapter explores in greater detail how the Forum functions in terms of membership, governance, finances and purposes.

2 Purposes public and private
How the Forum works

Membership and other forms of participation

This chapter examines how the World Economic Forum operates as an institution. It begins by looking at membership, the core element that defines the Forum's nature as a membership organization. The costs and benefits of different membership categories are considered, with particular focus on the increasingly important category of Strategic Partners. The section that follows discusses how the Forum is governed and managed and reviews the organization's finances. The subsequent section surveys the Forum's information output at a general level (for more details on the Forum's research see Chapter 5). The chapter concludes with a discussion of how the Forum organizes its conferences, including the Davos Annual Meeting.

Membership

In recent years the media have tended to reinforce the emergence of mixed popular perceptions of the World Economic Forum, including a substantial measure of "guilt by association" with other multilateral economic institutions embroiled in controversy, such as the World Trade Organization (WTO) over its trade liberalization agenda and the International Monetary Fund (IMF) over its Structural Adjustment Programs and "one size fits all" approach to public finance in developing countries. The Forum, however, is fundamentally unlike other multilateral economic institutions. The Forum is not and was never intended to be a public international organization. From its inception the organization was conceived as a private, not-for-profit foundation to promote the exchange of information and generation of ideas for the benefit of its members. Like other private societies, the Forum is self-selecting: its existing members choose whom to admit as new members. Its membership was initially comprised of European firms and gradually broadened to include as its potential member pool the "top 1200" global firms (criteria for inclusion being $1 billion in annual sales for firms, and management of $1 billion in capital for banks). The Forum had attracted 300 member firms by 1980, its fifth year as a membership organization. The number of members rose to 500 by 1985, 710 by 1990, and reached 1000 in 1994 (see Figure 2.1).

As the Forum's public role and visibility have grown, so too has the distinction between membership and non-membership. Up until 1993 top executives of non-member firms could attend the Davos meeting by paying a non-member attendance fee, but from 1993, in response to increasing pressure on space at Davos and members' concerns about the size of the meeting, the Forum began to limit attendance to member firms and Forum-invited guests only.[1] Since the Forum became a membership organization in 1976, member firms have borne the cost of funding the activities of the Foundation through an annual membership fee that in 2005 stood at SFr30,000/year, which does not include members' attendance fees for the meetings and summits themselves. For the price of a standard institutional membership, a firm currently receives one seat at the Davos annual meeting at the members' price, one free seat at each Forum regional activity for board members of the firm's headquarters, one complimentary copy of the annual *Global Competitiveness Report*, and access to other Forum documents and research publications as relevant.

The process of becoming a member of the World Economic Forum is competitive, as the Foundation took the decision in 1996 to limit the membership to 1000 firms. According to Managing Director Peter

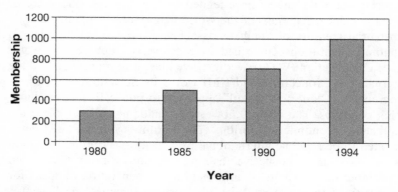

Figure 2.1 Growth in number of member firms in the World Economic Forum to present levels

Torreele, the Foundation has found 1000 to be a manageable number of members that can cover the globe and bring a sufficient level of input to the topics and issues under discussion at meetings. Just as some firms actively seek to join the Forum each year, at the same time the Forum staff and existing members are active in identifying firms that they wish to join their ranks. A membership committee reads the applications of prospective members each year, and two of every three applicants are rejected. The firms whose applications are rejected tend to be firms that apply again each year. Recruitment, on the other hand, is taken seriously. For example, recently the Forum successfully recruited the dynamic and rapidly expanding Chinese electronics firm Lenovo, which bought IBM's personal computer manufacturing business in 2005. The most effective method of recruitment, Forum managers have found, is to invite senior management of a target firm to attend a Davos summit as a guest of the Forum. A Forum summit, whether the annual meeting at Davos or one of the regional events, Peter Torreele explains, "is like sushi. It can't be described – it has to be tasted."[2] As a recruitment strategy, inviting sought-after potential members to Davos has been very successful. Of fifty potential member firms invited to attend the 2005 Annual Meeting, forty subsequently joined the Forum.

As of October 2005, the number of member firms stood at 961. Of these, 60 percent are global powerhouses with over $4 billion in annual revenue. Another 30 percent are smaller firms that dominate their region, such as the Indian firm Bajaj Auto. A further 10 percent are firms that are smaller still but have been invited to join because they have brought to market technologies and innovations that have shaken up the global economy, such as Google and eBay.[3] Membership in the Forum tends to be "leader-led," according to Managing Director Richard Samans: CEOs of firms usually make the decision whether a firm should become or remain a member of the Forum each year. The membership mix reflects both stability and freshness, as the core of the membership is comprised of long-term members, yet each year some 10 percent of member firms give up their membership. In 2005, 270 firms, or 28 percent of the total membership, had been members of the Forum for longer than ten years, and 536 firms, or 56 percent of the total membership, had been members for over five years.[4] The Forum, with reasonable justification, regards these figures as indicative of a high degree of member commitment to the organization, considering the upheaval in the global business environment over the past ten years. The rapid transformation of the global economic landscape since the end of the Cold War, the emergence and collapse of the internet bubble, and the increase in the pace of mergers and acquisitions have all had a significant impact upon the identity and financial position of firms that would be members of the Forum. Firms leave the Forum for three principal reasons: one third cease to be members due to a merger or acquisition changing their corporate status; the rest leave either because of a change in CEO (which occurs in member firms on average every three years) or because their senior management no longer see particular value in membership for the company. The health of the global economy in general and of particular firms also has an impact upon whether firms renew their membership each year.[5]

Partnerships

Available to the Forum's institutional members are more select tiers of participation known as Partnerships. Foremost amongst these are the Strategic Partners, of which there were forty-two at the time of writing.[6] The Managing Board selects firms to be Strategic Partners carefully, as Strategic Partners by their nature represent the image of the Forum. For a large global firm, to become a Strategic Partner represents a high-profile, public commitment to the Forum and its mission. It means becoming identified with the World Economic Forum, its objectives and its events at the highest, most visible level. The names and profiles of Strategic Partners are featured prominently on the Forum website. Strategic Partner firms paid SFr500,000 annually for the privilege in 2005, but the return on the added investment is considerable for the company that finds participation in the Forum to be an indispensable part of its own approach to strategic planning, public diplomacy or corporate social responsibility. If members in a general sense drive the agenda of the Forum's research and discursive output, Strategic Partners are granted the opportunity to have a much more direct say in planning the agendas of Forum summits, Initiatives and other events. A CEO of a Strategic Partner firm is able to decide to join a Forum mission to a particular country, for example, and request that particular topics be discussed with particular in-country interlocutors. Managers of Strategic Partner firms participate actively with Forum staff in programme planning for the Davos Annual Meeting and regional summits. Co-chairs of the summits, selected from Strategic Partner firms, in effect "own" the summit programs. Strategic Partner firms also benefit from a heightened profile at summits by preparing reports on particular issues of interest that are circulated to other Forum members for preparatory reading in advance of events. Whereas standard institutional membership entitles a firm to send one representative to Davos each year, usually either the CEO or another senior executive, in addition to the benefits of standard membership Strategic Partner firms are entitled to bring four additional staff members to Davos meetings at the member's price. But with added privileges come additional responsibilities: as being a Strategic Partner requires a substantial investment of time and effort for member firms, in addition to the cost involved, many firms will choose to be Strategic Partners over two, three or four annual meetings but not indefinitely.[7]

Firms choose to become Strategic Partners for different reasons, and often for overlapping sets of purposes. For example, Gary Shainberg, Vice President for Technology and Innovation at BT Group, said that BT attended their first Davos annual meeting as a Forum member in 2005 and were so impressed that they signed up to become a Strategic Partner, bearing out Peter Torreele's "sushi" theory of marketing the Forum. According to Shainberg, corporate social responsibility is important, but opportunities for visibility of the firm's brand and for networking were of the greatest value to the firm: "at the end of the day it's about brand awareness and business closing . . . [when you can] get to an event where your CEO sees nine counterparts, you can't beat that."[8] Deloitte, Touche Tomatsu has been a Strategic Partner of the Forum for over fifteen years. Deloitte managers remain enthusiastic about the Strategic Partner program. The firm gets a lot out of the relationship, one senior manager reported. "The more you participate, the more you get out of it."[9] According to a representative of a firm that became a Strategic Partner relatively recently, the firm benefited from being able to send a larger number of staff to Davos. He found the greatest value of Davos to be the networking opportunities, noting that in the months following the 2005 annual meeting he had already contacted individuals he had met at Davos to pursue further issues. This individual did not envisage the World Economic Forum as being part of his firm's corporate social responsibility strategy, observing that the firm had a very different, well developed approach to CSR.[10]

Several other types of partnerships are now available to members. Annual Meeting Partnerships, priced at SFr350,000 annually in 2005, entitle firms to a leadership role at the Davos Annual Meeting and two additional seats at Davos at the members' price.[11] Regional Partnerships offer a leadership role at one or more regional summits; Initiative Partnerships afford the opportunity to develop and take a leadership role in Forum Initiatives; and Industry Partnerships grant members access to specific industry-related Forum workstreams and contents. Each of these latter three categories of partnership was priced at SFr250,000 annually in 2005 and included one additional seat at the Davos meeting at the member's price. Two good examples are Cisco Systems and Computer Associates, already Strategic Partners, and who became Initiative Partners for the Jordan Education Initiative in 2003, giving senior management of both firms steering roles in planning and executing the work of the Initiative (see Tables 2.1 and 2.2).

Other types of membership

In recent years the Forum has created other types of memberships for firms and individuals who do not meet the standard large global firm criteria. Other categories of members are drawn from fast-growing firms developing cutting edge technologies, the Technology Pioneers, and younger leaders of business and other fields, the Young Global Leaders (YGLs). Between 30 and 50 firms doing groundbreaking work in biotechnology/healthcare, information and energy technologies are selected each year to be Technology Pioneers for a two-year term, which includes participation for their chief executives in the Davos meeting and other Forum summits and activities. As Technology Pioneers grow as firms over time, some may be invited to join the Forum as full members.[12] The Forum for Young Global Leaders, which succeeded the Global Leaders of Tomorrow program, is a group over 1000 dynamic individuals aged under forty, drawn from the ranks of global business, politics, journalism and civil society, who have already demonstrated leadership skills and a commitment to social entrepreneurship. The YGL Forum is headed by Nicole Schwab, Klaus and Hilde Schwab's daughter. Each year the World Economic Forum appoints between 200 and 300 YGLs to serve five-year terms participating in the activities of the Forum and meeting regularly to work on the Forum's "2020 Initiative," a research project aimed at identifying problems arising from the expected interaction of the global industrial and social environments in 2020 and creating proactive strategies to address those problems.[13] A related undertaking of the Forum is the Women Leaders Programme, which seeks to increase the participation of women in the Forum, its activities and events. The Women Leaders Programme also works to bring the Forum's knowledge resources to bear, through research and action, on improving global conditions of women and mobilizing the full participation of women in economic development (see Chapter 6 for further details on the Women Leaders Programme).[14]

Table 2.1 World Economic Forum membership categories with associated costs and privileges

Scheme	Cost	Main privileges
Membership	30,000 Sfr/year	One seat at member's price for Annual Meeting. One free seat at each regional activity for Board Members of Headquarters. One complimentary copy of *Global Competitiveness Report*. Access to other documents as relevant.
Institutional membership	30,000 Sfr/year	One free seat for Annual Meeting. One free seat at each regional activity for Board Members of Headquarters. One complimentary copy of *Global Competitiveness Report*. Access to other documents as relevant.
Regional partnership	250,000 Sfr/year	Membership and associated privileges. One additional seat at member's price for Annual Meeting. Involvement in one or more regional summits. Recognition scheme on one or more regional summits.
Initiative partnership	250,000 Sfr/year	Membership and associated privileges. One additional seat at member's price for Annual Meeting. Involvement in Initiative development. Recognition scheme in the framework of Initiative work.
Industry partnership	250,000 Sfr/year	Membership and associated privileges. One additional seat at member's price for Annual Meeting. Access to IP-specific workstreams and contents. One participant may attend the regional summit(s) where there is an Industry Partnership module, for free.
Annual Meeting partnership	350,000 Sfr/year	Membership and associated privileges. Two additional seats at member's price for Annual Meeting. Recognition scheme in the framework of Annual Meeting.

Continued on next page

Scheme	Cost	Main privileges
Strategic partnership	500,000 Sfr/year	Membership and associated privileges. Four additional seats at member's price for Annual Meeting. Involvement and acknowledgement as a partner in two regional summits and free seats for up to six participants at summits and three at roundtables. Involvement in Industry Partnership. Ten free seats at other regional events during the year. Recognition scheme in the framework of Forum activities.

Source: World Economic Forum.

Table 2.2 World Economic Forum Strategic Partners as of January 2006

ABB	Intel
Accel Partners	Investcorp
Accenture	JPMorgan Chase & Co.
AMD	KPMG
Apax Partners	Kudelski Group
Audi	Lehman Brothers
Avaya	Manpower
Bain & Company	Marsh & McLennan Companies
Barclays	McKinsey & Company
Bombardier	Merck & Co.
Booz Allen Hamilton	Merrill Lynch
BT	Microsoft Corporation
Cisco Systems	Nakheel
Citigroup	NASDAQ
The Coca-Cola Company	Nestlé
CA	New York Stock Exchange
Credit Suisse	Nike
Deloitte	PepsiCo
Deutsche Bank	Pfizer
Deutsche Telekom	PricewaterhouseCoopers
Deutsche Post World Net	Qatar Airways
Dubai Holding	Reliance Industries
Economic Development Board of Bahrain	Saudi Basic Industries Corporation (SABIC)
Ernst & Young	Siemens
Fluor Corporation	Swiss Re
Goldman Sachs	UBS
Google	Volkswagen

Source: World Economic Forum.

Communities

Other types of participation in the activities of the Forum beyond membership and partnership have been created more recently as well. From the Forum's practice of inviting guests to Davos and regional summits from amongst political leaders, media, academics, cultural leaders and other representatives of civil society has gradually evolved a set of groupings that the Forum now calls communities, which are organized entities for regular participation in the knowledge generation and problem solving activities of the Forum for certain categories of non-members. Fully organized communities do not encompass by any means the full range of invited participants to Forum events, but they have distinct identities, roles and responsibilities of their own. The Forum has given considerable thought to objectives for fostering and supporting the development of communities within the context of Forum activities. Selectivity of membership, a critical mass of numbers, frequent enough interaction to build personal relationships and learning, and rituals and symbols to facilitate building communities' identities are emphasized. Each community needs a manager to serve as its "concierge," and experts or "Sherpas" to assist primary community members. Significantly, each community should also benefit first from knowledge streams that it creates before they are disseminated to the rest of the Forum and, when appropriate, to the public.[15] For the Forum, turning groups of participants into communities was important because it redefined the possibilities and purposes of their participation. Creating structures for particular types of stakeholder to interact with one another potentially increases the value of their contribution to the overall multi-stakeholder dialogue.

Three communities provide participation for particular types of business leaders. The International Business Council (IBC) is a high-level advisory body made up of 100 CEOs and other senior executives tasked with identifying global business issues of concern and proposing solutions. Initiated in 2001, the IBC meets twice annually, at the Davos meeting and again during the summer. It also provides "intellectual stewardship to the World Economic Forum." A more region-specific version of the IBC, the Arab Business Council, was created in the aftermath of the invasion of Iraq specifically to facilitate a dialogue amongst Arab business leaders on how to improve economic competitiveness of Arab states and firms. A third business community, Industry Governors, is composed of leaders in five industrial sectors: basic industries; information, communication, and entertainment; consumer industries; financial services; and energy.

Industry Governors are leading the Forum's ongoing development of industry partnership groups intended to shape the global agenda on an industry-by-industry basis. Each industry partnership group meets privately at Davos during the Annual Meeting to generate ideas, many of which feed into new Forum Initiatives. For example, Industry Governors for the IT and communications sector meeting at Davos in January 2003 launched the Jordan Education Initiative.

Non-business communities include Global Foundation Leaders, made up of representatives of large charitable foundations, who advise the Forum on social investing. The group partners with the Synergos Institute, a New York-based CSO that describes itself as "dedicated to the development of effective, sustainable and locally based solutions to poverty," in providing information to Forum members on best practices in charitable giving to promote social gain. The Synergos Institute, like the Forum, is committed to the multi-stakeholder approach to achieving global development objectives.[16] Klaus and Hilde Schwab created the Schwab Foundation for Social Entrepreneurship in 1998 to bring together leading non-profit and for-profit social entrepreneurs from around the world in a community of best practice. Schwab Foundation members function as a knowledge network, meeting regularly at Forum meetings to exchange information and to be a resource for other Forum members and guests (see Chapter 5 for more on the Schwab Foundation).[17] On its website the Forum identifies three additional communities from civil society: Labour Leaders, Non-governmental Organizations, and Thought Leaders. The community of Thought Leaders breaks down into artists and cultural leaders, media leaders, religious leaders, and leaders from the world of sport. Whilst they are not as highly structured as the other communities, the Forum is targeting leaders in each of these communities to participate in Forum meetings and has convened meetings of each of these communities at Davos and other events. The organization of these communities is likely to develop along the lines of the already more formally structured communities over time.

Governance and management of the Foundation

The Forum is governed by the Foundation Board, a council of twenty representatives of member firms that meets three times a year, with intervening conferences by phone as needed. The Foundation Board reflects the Forum's commitment to the multi-stakeholder approach to governance. Board members, who serve three-year terms, are chosen from amongst leaders in business, politics, multilateral economic organizations, academia and civil society, and also reflect a considerable measure of geographical distribution by organization and nationality. At the time of writing, business leaders on the Board included Michael Dell, CEO of Dell, Nobuyuki Idei, Group CEO of Sony Corp., Pierer Heinrich, Chairman of the Supervisory Board, Siemens Corp., and Rajat Gupta, Senior Partner, McKinsey and Co. Political figures included Caio Koch-Weser, former German finance minister, Ernesto Zedillo Ponce de Leon, former president of Mexico, Flavio Cotti, former member of the Swiss Federal Council, and Queen Rania of Jordan. From multilateral economic organizations comes Peter Sutherland, former director general of the World Trade Organization (and now Chairman of Goldman Sachs International); from the media Niall FitzGerald, Chairman of Reuters Group; and from civil society Lord Carey of Clifton, former archbishop of Canterbury.

Primary duties of the Foundation Board in the current period include:

- managing the statutes of the World Economic Forum and its institutions;
- appointing new members;
- reviewing fund applications;
- determining and monitoring the execution of the World Economic Forum's strategies;
- defining the roles of the Managing Board and Committees, including the Mission Compliance Committee, which reviews policies, strategies and activities in light of the Forum's mission.[18]

In the Forum's early years the Foundation Board, two thirds of whom were required by Forum statutes to be nationals of or resident in Switzerland, tended to be individuals to whom Klaus Schwab was close and whom he trusted. Their functions included approving annual reports, approving the annual budget and establishing guidelines for managing Forum assets.[19] As the Forum has grown, the Board's role and independence has grown as well. Notwithstanding its role in governance of the Forum, the Foundation Board does not intervene in program-setting. It remains a principle of the Forum that its mission not be subjected to pressures either from outside influences or from its own members to act at variance with its institutional interests. This, according to Schwab, helps to preserve the Forum's intellectual integrity and credibility, which is one of its greatest strengths.[20]

The Forum has a permanent staff numbering around 200 working at its strikingly beautiful contemporary, sun-flooded headquarters on a hillside overlooking Lake Geneva in Cologny, a suburb of Geneva (Figure 2.2). Staffing has always been small, in 1980 numbering twenty-eight, including part-time workers, and as recently as 1992 only fifty-seven full-time and fifteen part-time staff were on the payroll. With many young and dynamic staffers, the Forum working atmosphere in the first decades was collegial and informal, and the organization remained non-hierarchical for many years, with all staff reporting directly to the Managing Director.[21] The Forum's senior managers have sought to keep the staffing lean even as the scope of the Forum's activities has continued to expand, in order to preserve the virtues of a short feedback and decisionmaking loop. Nonetheless, utilization of the Forum headquarters facility, only a few years old, has rapidly moved toward capacity.[22] This has led to plans for the opening of two permanent satellite offices for the Forum, in New York and Beijing (see Chapter 7).

The structure for management of the Forum's staff itself has varied over the institution's history. As it became clear from 1973 that the European Management Forum was solidly established as an ongoing institution, it was evident that it would not be possible for Klaus Schwab to develop the Forum at a strategic level and oversee all of its day-to-day operations at the same time. Up until 2000, the operations of the Forum were overseen by a single managing director. A succession of single managing directors, each long-serving, managed the business and the staff of the Forum as the institution grew, working closely with Schwab on a daily basis and thereby freeing him to lead the construction of the annual Davos agenda and develop new strategic directions for the Forum. In the summer of 2000, given the complex and interrelated nature of the global problems the Forum was addressing, the decision was taken that a collegiate approach drawing on the individual expertise of several managing directors would be more appropriate to the way that the Forum should do business. Hence power was distributed amongst a Managing Board of five managing directors. The shift to multiple managing directors was part of a broader management reorganization that included the establishment of three centres within the Forum to oversee different aspects of the organization's activities: the Centre for Global Industries to take charge of relations with members and partners; the Centre for Regional Strategies to oversee regional activities; and the Centre for the Global Agenda to take charge of the content creation of Forum events, public-private initiatives and the global competitiveness program.[23] Initially the Managing Board included one managing director who also served as chief executive officer, maintaining some of the functions that had been carried out

Figure 2.2a View from inside the Forum headquarters looking towards Lake
  Geneva. Photo: G.A. Pigman

Figure 2.2b View of the World Economic Forum headquarters building in
Cologny, Switzerland. Photo: G.A. Pigman

previously by the single managing directors. The last CEO, Jose Maria Figueres, a former president of Costa Rica, who had initially become a managing director in 2000, was appointed CEO in 2003 and then assumed additional leadership duties from Schwab in a January 2004 management reorganization. Following the departure of Figueres from the Forum in the fall of 2004 (see Chapter 6 for further details), Klaus Schwab has chaired the Managing Board, whilst Managing Director and Chief Operating Officer André Schneider assumed responsibility for organizational management.

Today's multi-member Managing Board comes from a broad range of professional backgrounds, areas of expertise and regions of the world. As the organization is small, the managing directors must work together daily, so getting along and being able to work as a team is essential. That this team spirit exists is evident to outsiders: discussing the objectives of the Forum and its approach to engaging with its critics over a relaxed luncheon in spring 2005 on a sunny outdoor terrace at a restaurant near the Forum's headquarters in Cologny, managing directors Ged Davis and André Schneider related easily to one another, discussing current business activities in a way that showed that they were in the same real-time information loop and engaging in an in-depth conversation with one another about key issues on an ongoing basis. At the same time they were able to step back and be reflective about how the Forum is perceived from outside and how it has engaged with its critics, bouncing ideas and thoughts off of one another with an ease and a comfort level that would be difficult to stage for the benefit of a visitor. Whilst perhaps not representative of every relationship amongst the managing directors, the way that Schneider and Davis interacted reflected well upon the management approach of the multi-member Managing Board.

The Forum regards the diversity of its Managing Board as one of its main strengths. Of the current managing directors at the time of writing, Managing Director and Chief Operating Officer André Schneider, a member of the Managing Board since 2003, was trained as a classical musician, receiving a Diploma from the Richard Strauss Konservatorium in Munich before going on to complete a Ph.D. in computer science at the University of Geneva. Schneider's career has spanned associations with several orchestras in Germany and Switzerland, as well as research, product development and consulting in the information technology field. Ged Davis, Managing Director and Head of the Forum's Centre for Strategic Insight, came to the Forum from a career in the energy industry. After obtaining advanced degrees in engineering and economics from the London School of

Economics and Stanford University, Davis worked for the Royal Dutch/Shell Group from 1972 until 2004, focusing on strategic planning roles that addressed Shell's role as a global corporate citizen. Davis has also produced forecasting scenarios for organizations ranging from the United Nations to the World Business Council for Sustainable Development on major issues of global concern, such as emissions and climate change, and AIDS in Africa. Richard Samans, Managing Director and Head of the Forum's Global Institute for Partnership and Governance, brought experience in the financial services industry and politics. After obtaining degrees in Economics, French and International Affairs from Tufts and Columbia Universities, Samans worked in corporate lending for Credit Lyonnais in New York, then held a series of legislative and policymaking posts in the US House of Representatives and Senate, eventually serving as Special Assistant to US President Bill Clinton for International Economic Policy from 1999 to 2001.[24]

Managing Director Peter Torreele has an extensive background in marketing and communications, which he uses to oversee the Forum's regional strategies and strategies for recruiting and retaining members. He holds degrees in engineering and economics, an MBA in marketing from Université Louvain-la-Neuve, and completed INSEAD's General Management Programme. Before joining the Forum Torreele held marketing positions at the Danone Group, the AlkenMaes Group and Roche Pharmaceuticals, whom he served as Global Head of Marketing for metabolism products at Roche Consumer Health. The Forum recruited its newest managing director, Michael Obermayer, in September 2005 to serve as Dean of the Global Leadership Fellows Programme, the Forum's newly established in-house education undertaking (see Chapter 7 for more details). With an M.Sc. in chemical engineering from the Royal Institute of Technology, Stockholm, an MBA from INSEAD, and a Ph.D. (summa cum laude) in biochemistry from the Max Planck Institute of Biochemistry and the University of Munich under his belt, Obermayer developed his career at McKinsey and Co. over more than twenty-five years, becoming a senior partner, establishing McKinsey's presence in Russia after 1989 and eventually serving as Chairman, McKinsey Eastern Europe from 1993 to 2000. Obermayer established the McKinsey Institute, McKinsey's global in-house corporate "university," where he "was instrumental in developing a state-of-the-art approach to organizational learning."[25] Table 2.3 below lists WEF's managing directors.

Serving on the management team under the managing directors is a compact cadre of individuals with functional and regional specializa-

Table 2.3 Managing directors of the World Economic Forum

Name	Appointed to Managing Board
André Schneider	2003
Richard Samans	2003
Ged Davis	2004
Peter Torreele	2004
Michael Obermayer	2005

tions. Four senior directors cover the areas of information technology, human resources, global risk, and financial services. Nineteen directors cover the Forum's major regions of activity (Africa, Asia, South Asia, Europe, Middle East), major industry sectors (consumer, energy, infrastructure, information and entertainment), major Forum programs and undertakings (partnerships, global competitiveness, global growth companies, International Business Council) and major functional responsibilities (communications and media, events, chief economist). Supporting the directors are sixteen associate directors.[26] As of 2005, the Forum's organizational structure was officially divided into six departments: Community Management, Community Development, the Centre for Public-Private Partnerships, the Centre for Strategic Insight, Communications, and Events and Resources Management.[27]

Finances

As a not-for-profit foundation, the governing financial principles of the Forum over its years of operation have been to raise sufficient funds from its operations to cover its operating costs and to finance growth and expansion as appropriate. In order for the Forum to maintain its intellectual independence, the organization needed to eschew any outside sponsorship or other ongoing funding relationships with public or private bodies. The Forum's original primary source of revenue was the fees charged to attendees of the Annual Meeting at Davos. Given the uncertainty in the early years over whether the Davos meeting would remain popular and well attended, and the resulting potential instability of that revenue stream, as well as the rising costs of putting on Davos each year, Schwab took the decision in 1976 to transform the European Management Forum into a membership organization. Annual membership fees became the second pillar of Forum revenues, which was to become crucial as the Forum steadily expanded the number of invited participants at Davos from the public sector and civil society. Later addition of two new categories of membership, Institutional Partners and Strategic Partners, offered higher levels of participation in the Forum for a substantially higher membership fee. Forum policy has been to pay the costs of attending Davos for invited guests, and, up until the mid-1980s, the Forum even paid modest honoraria to speakers of up to SFr5000.[28] A third, more modest revenue stream emerged later from the sale of the Forum's research products, such as the *Global Competitiveness Report* and *Global Agenda* magazine, to non-members of the Forum. Currently bringing in around SFr50,000 annually, sales of research publications have not been viewed by the Forum as a profit source but rather as an opportunity to disseminate their information content widely.

The Forum's financial strategy has been successful by any measure. From fiscal year 1973–4, the Forum has generated a financial surplus in every year except 1991–2, when they recorded a modest loss of SFr4623, resulting largely from investment in the ultimately unsuccessful WELCOM technology project (see Chapter 1).[29] By 2000, Davos summits were costing around $10 million to produce, but attendance fees were netting the Forum $12 million, of which the surplus goes towards the Foundation's ongoing expenses.[30] Whereas in 1982 Forum revenues stood at SFr7.7 million and costs at SFr7.5 million, by 1995–6 revenues had risen to SFr36.3 million and costs to SFr35.8 million, allowing the foundation's capital account to rise from SFr1.5 million to SFr4.7 million over the period. Nine years later, revenue stood at SFr83.3 million, costs at SFr82 million, and the capital account at SFr15.1 million. A healthy capital account has been crucial for the Forum, in that it has permitted the organization to maintain independence, remain debt-free and to fund major expansions of operations as required from its own resources. Financial independence has also placed the Forum in a unique position relative to many other CSOs that are large enough to function as diplomatic actors in their own right. As diplomatic actors, most CSOs, such as the International Committee of the Red Cross or Médecins Sans Frontières, face limitations as to how effectively and aggressively they can represent and advance the interests of their core constituency or membership, as they are often dependent at least in part for financial support from governments or multilateral organizations with which they must also engage or negotiate on substantive questions, e.g. how and where to distribute aid or the need for government or international intervention against atrocities. The World Economic Forum, by contrast, is free both to advance the particular interests of its members and to construct its own identity and develop and advance its own unique interests through discourse with other interlocutors without a material constraint. This advantage can be understood as a significant power resource, of which perhaps the Forum and its members are only beginning to become fully aware.

Key Forum financial data for 1994–2004 are shown in Figures 2.3 and 2.4.

Information output

As the core function of the Forum is to create and exchange knowledge and information, its primary output is the knowledge and information created. That information is created both for the global public and for the private use of its member firms. The tendency of the public to evaluate the Forum by criteria applicable to public international organizations rather than private institutions reflects the Janus face of the Forum's information output and the implicit ambiguity therein regarding how the organization wishes to be perceived. The Forum's public information function, which it has done an ever better job of marketing as communications technology has improved, is to bring together business leaders with other stakeholders in global society to

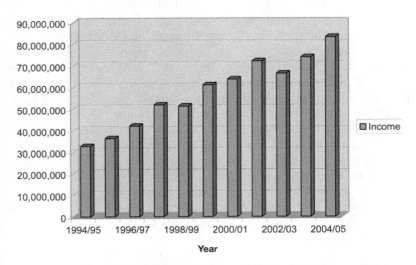

Figure 2.3 World Economic Forum key financial data: Total income (SFr) 1994–2004

Source: World Economic Forum Annual Report 2004–5

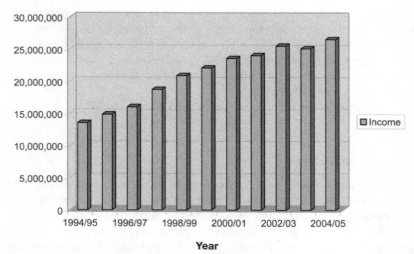

Figure 2.4 World Economic Forum key financial data: Income from members' fees (SFr) 1994–2004

Source: World Economic Forum Annual Report 2004–5

discuss major issues and problems of public and business policy, to exchange information, share knowledge and generate ideas for solving economic, social and political problems of all sizes. In the first few years Forum public information activities were confined largely to the Davos annual meetings and at first were dominated by business leaders, but the scope of the meetings rapidly increased to encompass public officials and representatives of civil society. The frequency of meetings also grew to include regional summits occurring on a near-monthly basis, and special initiatives such as that which produced the Europe-Asia dialogue and the Jordan Education Initiative.

Beyond meetings, the Forum has expanded its information output to include production of research, of which the most visible has been an annual series of research reports, which are published in conjunction with major commercial publishing houses. These series include the *Global Competitiveness Report* and several regional and functional series such as the *European Competitiveness and Transition Report*, the *Arab World Competitiveness Report*, and the *Global Information Technology Report*. The *Global Competitiveness Report*, which the Forum began publishing in 1979, contains league tables assessing different metrics of competitiveness of around half of the world's independent states, as well as explanatory discussion and analysis, and a collection of scholarly articles by leading academics and businesspeople addressing current issues relating to competitiveness. In addition to the annual series, the Forum publishes one-off research reports on globally important topics, such as the 2005 *Women's Empowerment: Measuring the Global Gender Gap*. The Forum has also sponsored the publication of scholarly books, such as *Corporate Governance and Capital Flows in a Global Economy*, edited by Peter K. Cornelius and Bruce Kogut and published in conjunction with Oxford University Press in 2003. The book was one of the end products of the Corporate Governance Initiative, a research initiative that the Forum undertook in response to the "Kleptogate" financial scandals beginning in 2000 that affected firms such as Enron, WorldCom, HealthSouth, and Adelphia Communications, among others, in the United States, and Parmalat in Europe. (For more information on Forum research, see Chapter 4.) Box 2.1 lists WEF's current annual publications.

Non-members of the Forum may purchase major Forum reports and publications, such as the *Global Competitiveness Report* and the scholarly books, whilst many other more compact research reports, such as *Women's Empowerment: Measuring the Gender Gap*, are available free on the Forum website. Members of the Forum receive Forum research publications as a privilege of membership. The remainder of the Forum's private information function has centred around creation of networks and a database through which members could exchange information amongst themselves. These networks function throughout the year as well as at the summits and meetings themselves through,

---

Box 2.1: World Economic Forum annual publications as of January 2006

Annual Report
Newsletter
Annual Meeting Report
Regional Summit reports
Global Competitiveness Report
Global Competitiveness Programme Executive Opinion Survey
Africa Competitiveness Report
Arab World Competitiveness Report
Global Information Technology Report
Women's Empowerment: Measuring the Global Gender Gap

among other things, a "members only" intranet site within the publicly accessible Forum website. The Forum pioneered the use of information networking technology to connect Davos participants to one another during the actual meetings, a service that enhanced the value of participating in the Annual Meeting to members and has become progressively more useful as information technology became more sophisticated. One of the most useful information resources that Forum members and other attendees of Davos and other Forum meetings receive is the hard-copy "facebook" of meeting participants, in which the name, photo, brief biography and all-important contact details of each participant appear. Having the facebook to hand after a meeting facilitates the keeping up of contacts made at meetings and makes it possible for attendees to reach out to other attendees whom they might not have met but might have heard speak on a panel or with whom they might have a common interest.

This highlights the importance of the Forum's private information function of giving its corporate members venues to meet with one another and, with their invited guests from other spheres of public life, to discuss issues and problems. The private information exchanged in these settings, when circumstances are propitious, regularly lead to the making of private business deals. Frequently the Davos meeting and, in later years, the Forum regional summits, provide the only opportunity during the year when high-level executives of major global firms have the opportunity to see one other in an informal setting.[31] Where the public and private faces of the Forum's information output can be seen to converge is in the Forum's distinctive mechanism for bringing about change in the public policy arena. The principal way that change occurs as a result of Forum activities is when its members and participants act, in their particular spheres of operation public or private, national or transnational, upon ideas or understandings that they have gleaned by participating in Forum meetings, networks and communities. In 2000, for example, PricewaterhouseCoopers (PWC) CEO James J. Schiro, who served as Co-chairman of the 1999 Davos Annual Meeting, wrote on the PWC website of how he gained an appreciation of the urgency for CEOs to become more internet-literate if firms are to make e-business initiatives successful. Schiro reported that discussions he had at Davos illuminated the findings of a Forum Global CEO Survey revealing a lack of internet literacy amongst CEOs of global firms. The survey findings and discussions that flowed therefrom at Davos also highlighted for Schiro the importance of coordinating technology strategies with "listening to customers" and "assessing the nuances of local business ecologies:" "technology tools work best when they are deployed by people operating in the context of well understood values, abilities, and motivations. The modern and the timeless support each other in today's global enterprise."[32]

Organizing conferences

Notwithstanding the Forum's steady expansion of the scope of its activities and projects, the function most closely associated with its core identity remains hosting the Annual Meeting at Davos. Organizing the Davos meeting and the regional summits is a complex task that goes on throughout the year, and it is something that the Forum has come to be known for doing exceptionally well. Content planning and operational/logistical organization are related but distinct projects. In terms of content, the Foundation managers work with senior executives of Forum member firms on an ongoing basis to identify important issues and questions to be discussed at Davos and the annual regional meetings. The Forum, however, retains ownership of the overall summit agendas, and Klaus Schwab continues to take a lead role in the agenda development process. An eight-person "programme development team" on the permanent staff works throughout the year to monitor issues and draw up the issue agenda for the year's Davos summit.

In 2005 member firms paid attendance fees amounting to 15.6 million Swiss francs to attend the 2005 Davos Annual Meeting. Whereas member firms of the Forum pay a fee to attend Davos meetings and regional summits (in addition to their annual membership fees), non-members are invited to attend to participate as interlocutors as guests of the Forum. Invited guests acquire no automatic entitlement to attend subsequent meetings, although some guests, such as Bill Clinton, are invited back year after year. The Forum staff choose the guest list for each meeting based on the topics to be discussed and who is likely to make the most useful contributions to the discussions. Managing Director Peter Torreele describes the process of putting together the list of invited guests for an annual meeting as akin to the way a good chef picks the right ingredients for a fine meal: it is not an exact science, sometimes involving a considerable amount of trial and error.[33]

Whilst Forum staff manage the content of the summits, they outsource operational and logistical requirements for the summits and regional meetings. The Forum contracts with Publicis Events, a Paris-based firm employing twenty dedicated full-time workers in Geneva, to run the Davos meetings. The number of staff working on the Annual Meeting gradually rises to around 300 by early January and then rises sharply to around 2,000 employed in the last week of January for the meeting itself. The Forum itself employs 430 workers at Davos, including the bulk of its full-time workforce, who focus exclusively upon Davos for varying periods of time leading up to and during the meeting, as well as students employed for the event itself. Publicis staff rises to 180, including the employment of part-time students. Subcontractors to Publicis employ 760 people. The Forum uses a number of partner firms to provide services at the Annual Meeting, particularly in the information technology area: support for the "Davos Companion" iPAQ handheld information devices for attendees, projection services for plenary and panel sessions, electronic polling, and related needs. These firms employ 150 staff. Last but not least, security firms employ over 300 to provide surveillance and protection during the meeting, not a small task given that routinely some of the most heavily protected global political leaders, such as the presidents of the United States and Pakistan and the prime ministers of Israel and India, are invited to attend. Staffing levels for 2006 are shown in Figure 2.5.

The Forum staff designed the Davos experience for members and invited guests carefully to optimize the quality of the time spent at the

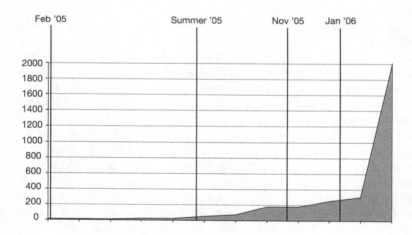

Figure 2.5 World Economic Forum staffing levels preparing for the Annual Meeting 2006. Total number of staff who work at Davos: WEF staff, permanent staff who work for Publicis, temporary staff hired for the occasion

Source: World Economic Forum

conference for all the participants. The small size of the village of Davos, its distance from major urban centres and facilities, and its relative inaccessibility from major airports, mainline railways and motorways impose major structural limitations on how a conference such as the Forum's Annual Meeting can be run, the most significant of which is an absolute limit on the potential number of attendees and support staff. With over 4000 members, guests and staff spending the better part of a week in Davos, catering and other logistical demands are enormous. Around 40,000 meals are served, and 100 limousines are used to transport members and guests to (and occasionally within) the Davos venue. The physical limitations of Davos are an important, but by no means the only, reason behind the Forum's decision to limit attendance at Davos to CEOs of member firms and to invited guests only. One of the practical consequences of asking CEOs of firms and heads of government to attend a multi-day conference without their customary retinue of support staff is that Forum and support staff must provide sufficiently for their needs and comfort during their stay at Davos, which likely raises the number of staff that the Forum needs to provide. Eventually some exceptions to the "principals only" policy developed. From the 1990s spouses of attendees were permitted to accompany their partners to Davos and to attend non-private events, including social functions. When the Forum created Strategic Partners as a new category of membership in the 1990s, one of the rewards for Strategic Partners' substantially higher membership fees was the opportunity to send five attendees instead of one (see above).

These relatively minor exceptions notwithstanding, the "principals only" attendance policy lies at the core of the Forum's conception of how the Annual Meeting should function as a venue for communication, information exchange and problem solving. From the early years of the Forum, a key component of Schwab's vision of the type of interaction that would take place at annual meetings was the idea that participants would be given the opportunity, and indeed the obligation, to speak for themselves, directly, to other participants. Being unable to have aides and assistants present would remove the possibility of formulation of "official" responses to questions and positions in debates. The organizational format of "live" panel discussions made it difficult, if not impossible, for attendees to coordinate their comments and participation with their home bases in real time. Some events, such as the Global Town Hall Meeting that opens the Davos Annual Meeting, require participants to register opinions on issues being discussed in real time using electronic polling equipment. Constructing the discourse to take place in such an unmediated way was bound to produce a different quality of affect. Individuals would come to know one another as individuals. There would be an opportunity for participants to become more familiar with each other's backgrounds and develop a greater understanding of the context in which each other's views on issues of common concern developed. Through shared social interactions as well as formal panel discussions, conditions would be created for participants to re-evaluate and potentially reconstruct their own interests and positions, which could facilitate the reaching of agreement on common approaches to solving problems that had hitherto divided different groups of interlocutors. As part of his Theory of Communicative Action, German social theorist Jürgen Habermas articulated the idea that sharing a *Lebenswelt*, or lifeworld, was one of the factors that could increase the possibility that negotiators with different positions could reach agreement. Creation of a *Lebenswelt* for participants to a negotiation where the participants had not previously shared one was a technique for improving the prospects of successful conflict resolution. The conditions of Davos, especially for those who have the opportunity to return year after year to renew and deepen acquaintances, can be seen as the sort of *Lebenswelt* that Habermas and scholars in his tradition would identify as particularly useful to improving the possibility of communication over difficult issues.[34]

Preparing the groundwork for discussion of the current activities, issues, debates and criticisms of the World Economic Forum in the latter half of the book, the next chapter examines the Forum's unique boundary-crossing nature in the context of major theoretical debates in contemporary global affairs: ideational vs. material causation, classical vs. contemporary diplomacy, public vs. private actors, and competing narratives of institutional identity.

3 The Forum in contemporary global society

Theoretical questions

The Forum as a contemporary international organization

This chapter frames the discussion of the current activities, issues, debates and criticisms of the World Economic Forum that follow in subsequent chapters by reflecting on the unique character of the Forum and its intellectual implications for understanding contemporary global affairs. The Forum exists as an international organization in a global landscape of contemporary actors that is becoming steadily more crowded with ever more types of actors. Yet the Forum can legitimately lay claim to being unique in terms of what it is and what it does. By studying the Forum we can gain understandings of contemporary global interaction that are not readily available by studying other bodies. As was noted in the Introduction, the Forum is by its nature a boundary-crossing institution. Its boundary-crossing nature makes it an ideal vehicle for understanding, and for deconstructing, key intellectual boundaries in our understanding of global affairs: ideational vs. material causation, classical vs. contemporary diplomacy, public vs. private actors, and competing narratives of institutional identity.

Ideational vs. material causation

The World Economic Forum is about nothing if it is not about knowledge and ideas: their creation, development and dissemination. But the relationship between ideas and global change – social, economic and political – is less transparent and more controversial. One of the long-running debates amongst scholars of international relations, political science and sociology has concerned the relative importance of material and ideational factors in explaining and understanding causation: what makes actors behave in the way that they do? Traditional

Marxian understandings view the interests of actors as determined by their position in the economic structure of society: their relationship to the dominant mode of production. The structure of the economy, by indicating the interests of actors, gives a strong indication of what choices they will make. Owners of capital will seek to maximize profit by extracting the maximum surplus value from labor. Workers will seek to retain the full value of their labor power, if necessary by seizing ownership of the means of production. Neoclassical economics echoes this structurally based understanding of economic behaviour with its "rational actor" assumption. In a market economy, an individual, a firm or a government will act rationally to maximize its utility function. To understand the behaviour of governments of nation-states in the international system, neorealist and neoliberal scholars of international relations debate the relative importance of systemic incentives to compete or best one's rivals vs. systemic incentives to cooperate. Multilateral institutions emerged and have succeeded in the international system, according to neoliberals, because they have facilitated cooperation, which has been in the "rational actor" interest of governments.

Yet structural explanations for the behaviour of governments, firms, individuals and other actors in global society have been felt by many contemporary scholars to be inadequate. Too often in history, they have not proved to be accurate. Just as many interests expressly articulated by actors appear irreducible to economic motivations, actors often are observed to make choices that do not appear in accord with either their stated or their structurally deduced interests. More contemporary, post-positivist approaches to this "structure-agent" problem have sought to conceptualize a more interactive relationship between structural influences and agency in understanding social and economic behaviour. Critics of neoclassical economics have undermined the power of the rational actor assumption by highlighting actors' lack of access to full information required to make rational decisions and have argued that rationality itself is "bounded," as evidenced by the frequent lack of transitivity of actors' preference orderings. Social constructivist scholars contend that interests, far from being fixed by an actor's position in the economic structure, are learned and re-learned through social interaction. The desires and taste preferences upon which interests are formed are themselves subject to modification through contact with and influence by other actors.[1] Into these processes of social construction of desires and interests structural factors may enter, but equally there is room for ideas to arise, become shared, and, sometimes, to have a life of their own. By coming into contact with different ideas, and through discursive interaction with other actors, actors can come to understand their own interests differently, and act upon their reconstructed interests accordingly.

It is this social space for the developing and debating of ideas and reconstructing of interests, economic and otherwise, that the World Economic Forum occupies so compellingly. Members of the Forum publicly state that they attend the Davos annual meeting and other meetings to hear and discuss new ideas. Invited participants from politics and civil society attend Forum meetings and summits as a way to share their own perspectives, agendas and interests with Forum members and other attendees, in the hope of attracting interest and support; in the process their pre-existing interests and agendas may be reconstructed as well. For example, the idea of social entrepreneurship – building businesses that through their processes and products create and promote public goods and social values – has been steadily foregrounded and normalized at the Forum's meetings and summits, and more recently through the creation and development of the Schwab Foundation for Social Entrepreneurship. Recognizing and publicly rewarding standards of best practice for social entrepreneurship, as the Schwab Foundation now does by presenting its Social Entrepreneur of the Year awards at Forum meetings, promotes socially aware norms of practice in the broader global business community. Whilst the Forum is by no means the only institution to promote social entrepreneurship, Forum meetings do constitute a particularly effective venue for integrating social entrepreneurship into the overall interest perceptions of Forum member firms.

Classical vs. contemporary diplomacy

The representations and communications that take place at meetings and summits of the World Economic Forum involve building interpersonal relationships, thinking about the future, solving problems, resolving disagreements. The interactions take place between the principals, or high-ranking emissaries from the principals, of large global firms, governments large and small, multilateral economic institutions and NGOs. At many of the meetings "Track I" diplomacy takes place: high-level negotiation of an ongoing dispute or conflict between interested parties, be they the prime ministers of East and West Germany, the Prime Minister of Turkey and the CEO of Chevron, or the President of the United States and the CEO of Microsoft. The diplomatic function of the Forum raises questions about the nature of contemporary diplomacy and the actors that engage in it. Scholars of diplomacy traditionally have understood diplomacy as "the dialogue between states," focusing upon interactions between the sovereigns of nation-states, through their accredited representatives, predominantly concerning issues of *haute politique*: security, defence, territory and control of resources.[2] The range of representations, communications and negotiations that took place between the superpowers and between their allies during the Cold War, from the high-tension negotiations of the Cuban Missile Crisis to the détente of the Nixon-Brezhnev years, is emblematic of this classical understanding of diplomacy.

Following the end of the Cold War and the increased visibility of global economic competition, other scholars have sought to think about diplomacy differently, highlighting that diplomacy as it has been practiced down through history has in fact always been focused on the economic, the social and the cultural as much as it has been upon military and security issues. This approach has regarded the classical view of diplomacy as reifying and reinforcing intellectual boundaries between the domestic and the international, the public and the private, and the political and the economic, all of which get in the way of a clear understanding of contemporary diplomatic practice.[3] This same critical approach to diplomacy also challenges the classical view that only governments of nation-states are diplomatic actors, arguing that contemporary diplomacy engages not only governments but large global firms such as Shell and Microsoft, and major transnational civil society organizations such as Médecins Sans Frontières and Greenpeace. Although not functionally identical to nation-states, these actors engage in the core, generic diplomatic functions of representation and communication in ways that are similar enough to those of nation-state governments that it is more useful to understand the landscape of diplomatic interaction as including them than not. Another group of diplomatic actors that falls under this rubric is multilateral institutions, ranging from international financial institutions, such as the World Bank and the International Monetary Fund, to multilateral political institutions such as the United Nations. These institutions, a product of the changing global political and economic environment of the second half of the twentieth century, have themselves gradually made a transition from functioning solely as venues for diplomacy between their member governments to acquiring a distinct diplomatic personality of their own: to becoming diplomatic actors in their own right, with interests, agendas and priorities that are distinct from the mere aggregation of those of their member governments.[4]

Critical scholars of contemporary diplomacy also focus upon the impact of the revolution in information and communications technologies (ICTs) upon the processes of diplomacy, ranging from acceleration in the speed of diplomatic communications, which can either facilitate swifter resolution of disputes, or increase the risk of their escalation by denying actors sufficient time to reflect and respond in a measured way. Greater use of multiple channels of communication in real time may disintermediate diplomacy by reducing the need for embassies and missions. Perhaps the most significant way that technology has affected diplomacy is by heightening the importance of public diplomacy. Global publics, once informed, increasingly have the power to confer legitimacy upon, or with draw it from, policies of governments and firms. By increasing the ability of global publics to acquire and evaluate information for themselves and by limiting the ability of governments and firms to conduct diplomacy in secret, ICTs have heightened the need for governments, firms and civil society organizations to communicate effectively to global publics. Public diplomacy, the set of techniques and approaches for this type of diplomatic communication, has been transformed substantially in recent years by new ICTs, and those actors that have been swift to adapt them to their public diplomacy needs effectively have reaped rewards accordingly.

In this new and unfamiliar (at least to some) landscape of contemporary diplomacy, the World Economic Forum once again occupies a unique space. Despite being an institution whose membership is not of governments, like other multilateral institutions the Forum serves as a venue for diplomacy. By the 1980s, the Forum had become a venue for a broad range of diplomatic communications, from the more formal discussions between leaders of Greece and Turkey, East and West Germany, Israel and Palestine to more informal but equally important discussions between North and South Korean officials, to meetings between heads of government and CEOs of global firms, to meetings between CEOs and heads of civil society organizations. Yet from the start, the Forum was never only a neutral venue in which diplomatic interaction could happen. From the moment they decided to respond to the 1973 oil crisis and Yom Kippur War in a particular positive manner, Klaus Schwab and the other senior managers of the Forum had certain broad interests that they sought to use the Forum to further. These interests were constructed in part through consultation with the Forum's subscribing members, but they were also based upon a particular set of values concerning global society and the global economy, which Schwab brought to bear from the start by the act of founding the Forum: values such as combining entrepreneurship with serving the global public good, and cooperation in resolving disputes. The Forum began to invite political leaders, and later civil society leaders, to Forum meetings specifically to encourage the types of diplomatic interactions that would result in the creation of a better global economic, political, social and thus indeed business climate. Subsequently the Forum began responding to particular political conflicts by inviting pairs of leaders or officials to Davos when they saw an opportunity for that venue to contribute to the process of conflict resolution. Davos provides an environment that is highly supportive, without creating the pressure of an official, results-oriented bilateral summit. When Forum-sponsored diplomacy achieves results, Forum members benefit, either directly or indirectly, and the Forum itself benefits, both through enhancement of its reputation and by having furthered its own institutional diplomatic objectives. Hence the Forum is quintessentially an international organization that is both a venue for diplomacy and a diplomatic actor in its own right.

The Forum has also been a leader in the adoption of new technologies for communication and sharing information, both between its members themselves and between the Forum and the global public. Schwab has always placed a priority upon deploying the latest technologies, even if it has meant making some technology experiments that have not been successful, as the case of WELCOM showed. From the start the strength of the Forum as an organization was as a knowledge network of members, and subsequently it has become a network of networks that connect its members to each other and to the different interlocutors and communities who participate in Forum events and activities. The speed at which and ease with which participants in the Forum's networks can communicate has accelerated dramatically with the development of the internet, and with the Forum's proprietary channels for gathering and disseminating information and research. Use of electronic polling at meetings is an example. The Forum has also been ahead of the curve in using technology to develop its own public diplomacy, communicating information about itself and its objectives to the global public. At a time when many international organizations were struggling to understand how to design a website that was attractive, user-friendly, informative and that left the reader with a positive impression, the Forum's use of the internet in the 1990s to tell its story to the global public was so successful at telling the world about the Forum that it informed critics as well as supporters and the neutral public about its activities and objectives (see Chapters 1 and 6). This left the Forum faced with the broken feedback loop problem that is common in contemporary public diplomacy: the realization that the message being received is at least in part not the same as the message being transmitted, and the challenge of adjusting the message so it is received in the desired way.

Problematizing boundaries between public and private

One dominant theme in contemporary global studies is the blurring and breaking down of boundaries between what has traditionally been understood as the public and the private. This has taken place in a variety of ways. The "public" has become more "private" through decisions such as the privatization of traditional government functions such as provision of public utilities, outsourcing of tasks historically done by government (such as road building and repair), delivery of social services, and aspects of military and civil security provision. On the other hand, the "public" has entered traditionally "private" space as governments have become involved in financing research and development of leading-edge technologies, including taking ownership stakes in technology-intensive businesses. This notion of "public-private partnerships" encapsulates the blending of roles traditionally viewed as separate, both by adherents of classical market economics and Marxian social ownership of the means of production. At the personal level, changing perceived security requirements have made private individuals in many cases much more accepting of increased government surveillance over their movements, their possessions, and their business transactions, particularly those that take place in cyberspace.

Perhaps no global organization today better encapsulates this problematizing of the boundaries between public and private than the World Economic Forum. The Forum is a very private institution with a very public agenda. Its core missions centre around building communication between private and public officials and around creating and sustaining public-private partnerships. According to Managing Director Richard Samans, there is a "creative tension" between the public and the private at the Forum. Striking the right balance between public and private, finding the "sweet spot," according to Samans, necessitates a process of intellectual give and take, which Forum staff pursue informally and through innovation. There is "not a long playbook" available to provide guidance on getting the balance right, Samans commented.[5] Managing Director Ged Davis argues that public-private partnerships are crucial, since given the complexity of global issues neither government nor business nor civil society has sufficient perspective and understanding to solve major regional or global problems on their own. Davis sees the Forum as the platform on which public-private partnerships can take place.[6]

Public-private partnerships are anything but new in historical terms, and examples abound, ranging from parliamentary-chartered firms such as the British and Dutch East India companies being granted exclusive development and trading rights in the eighteenth century to the coordinated participation of major North American and European firms in the Marshall Plan-funded reconstruction of Europe after World War II. However, the origins, design and management of public-private partnerships in recent decades have all begun to change concurrently with the blurring of boundaries between public and private. The Forum can be seen as at the centre of these changes. Klaus Schwab's multi-stakeholder approach to global problem solving and governance, which the Forum has been unfolding and developing for over three decades now, is a sort of template for the evolution of public-private cooperation. Ideas may originate from any category of stakeholder, or combination of stakeholder, and will likely require the coordination and participation of several types of stakeholder to be implemented successfully. The Forum's Disaster Resource Network (DRN), one of the Forum's more recent and already successful Initiatives (see Chapter 5 on the Initiatives), is a good example. Following the vast destruction and huge loss of life resulting from an earthquake that occurred in Gujarat during the 2001 Annual Meeting, senior executives of construction and logistics firms meeting at Davos discussed how they could cooperate in the aftermath of future natural disasters to facilitate the delivery of supplies and more rapid reconstruction efforts. They created the DRN to be a network to facilitate the identification and rapid meeting of needs. The network, in order to function, required the participation not only of firms, but of governments in disaster-affected areas and CSOs involved in relief and reconstruction efforts. The Forum, with its existing network infrastructure of top-level contacts across all the relevant stakeholders, was ideally positioned to act as facilitator of the network.

Another aspect of the blurring of public-private boundaries revealed by the Forum is the question of inclusion and exclusion: who is invited to participate in Forum events, and who is not. Small size is a crucial determinant of how knowledge can be generated and exchanged at formal panels and through informal gatherings and interactions. Forum events at their core are about who is present, because who is present determines what ideas are discussed, how they are debated and shaped, and what possible uses and outcomes are envisioned and undertaken at the conclusion. Thus, by extension, who is excluded precludes intellectual and imaginative possibilities that otherwise might have taken form. From 2000, the Forum responded to demands by its critics for greater access to and participation in Forum events in a number of ways: increasing the number of civil society organizations invited to participate in Davos and other meetings, holding Open Forum meetings at Davos for the public to debate issues being considered by the delegates at the Annual Meeting, and sponsoring the Forum weblog (blog) on the Forum website (see Chapter 6 for further details). This has had the effect of involving a broader, more representative range of interests in the generation of the Forum's discursive contribution to global problem solving and, by extension, global governance, whilst still not putting it in a position to be able to claim a mantle of global legitimacy as representative of global civil society as a whole.

Competing narratives of institutional identity

One of the most interesting aspects of the story of the World Economic Forum is the way in which it illustrates how the identity of a transnational institution on the global stage is created, emerges and evolves. Like that of a nation-state or a private firm, the identity of the Forum has come to be recognized as a result of the interplay between competing narratives of its evolution: stories of how and why the Forum was created and has developed, as told by the Forum itself and as told by others. The identity of an institution may be least interesting when it is least contested: when there is general agreement about who and what the institution is between those who are members of or work for the institution and those outside of the institution, whom the institution serves, or with whom the institution interacts. Yet the identities of most significant organizations are at least in some respects contested; hence to explore competing narratives of the evolution of an institution yields a richer understanding of the institution and how it interacts with the rest of the world. The most significant contrast amongst narratives must lie between the internal narrative of the institution itself and those external narratives told by others. Two external narratives of the evolution of the World Economic Forum already mentioned (see Introduction) are the Shar-pei, which can be embraced by adherents of neoliberal globalization, and the Wolf in Sheep's Clothing, adopted by alter-globalizers and other critics of neoliberal globalization. There are other narratives as well. The discussion that follows contrasts the internal evolutionary narrative told by the Forum itself with those narratives recounted by those with whom the Forum interacts.

How does the World Economic Forum identify itself? How does the organization represent itself to itself and to outsiders? One of the principal ways that the Forum identifies itself is as a civil society (or non-governmental) organization, which may seem surprising to those accustomed to thinking first of organizations like the Red Cross or Friends of the Earth when CSOs are mentioned. Yet the Forum has official non-governmental organization (NGO) consultative status with the UN Economic and Social Council. But going deeper, the Forum over its history has created a series of mission statements that track the evolution of its identity as it has grown from an organization tailored to the needs of European businesses to an institution promoting a multi-stakeholder approach to global problem solving and governance. In 1976 the EMF described itself as "an independent, self-supporting, non-profit foundation dedicated to the strategic needs of Europe's leading business decision makers."[7] By 1983 the mission proclaimed was more ambitious and more specific:

> Our mission is to provide the world economy with a continuous, independent and informal forum, where those who exercise the highest responsibilities in economic affairs can meet to exchange information, opinions and experience, to propose actions and elaborate projects, and to advance their common efforts for worldwide economic progress and cooperation.[8]

A decade later, the Forum's mission statement had evolved into a triumphal claim of success at its undertakings: "The World Economic Forum is the world's foremost institution integrating leaders from business, government and the sciences into a global partnership for economic and social progress."[9] In 2005 the Forum's promotional brochure leads off with a concise mission statement that highlights the Forum's role in discursive construction through agenda-shaping: "The World Economic Forum is an independent international organization committed to improving the state of the world by engaging leaders in partnerships to shape the global, regional and industry agendas."[10] On the Forum's blog, a site open to the internet-surfing public to respond to and comment on Forum issues, appears a slightly more descriptive header conveying the same general message:

> The World Economic Forum is an independent international organization committed to improving the state of the world. The Forum provides a collaborative framework for the world's leaders

to address global issues, engaging particularly its corporate members in global citizenship.[11]

From these evolving mission statements the Forum has derived several pithier mottos, or discursive identifying "tags." The most visible of these forms part of the Forum's logo, a curving arc running through the words "WORLD ECONOMIC FORUM" evoking the curvature of the Earth as viewed from space. Beneath the arc the ubiquitous caption, a simple if ambitious statement of objective: "Committed to improving the state of the world." The logo was designed by Pentagram, London, in 1987 (see Figure 3.1). Another widely used motto first introduced in 1989, which heads up the "About Us" section of the Forum website, is "Entrepreneurship in the global public interest."[12] This notion succinctly seats the objectives of business within Schwab's broader multi-stakeholder conception of global public affairs. In the same section of the website, the Forum is described as "the foremost community of world leaders" and is followed by a paragraph discussing the categories of members and communities participating in the Forum's activities.

The Forum's 2005 promotional brochure itself is a visually stunning presentation of the identity themes advanced through the mission

Figure 3.1 World Economic Forum logo, designed by Pentagram, London, 1987

statements and discursive tags. Featuring the curving globe logo on its lustrous gray cover, on each of its thirteen pages the brochure contains a rich color photo of scenes from around the world that reiterates the Forum's globe motif, which represents the positive associations of global economy, global society and global governance: an ancient amphitheatre; a giant astronomical ground station "dish;" an overhead view of a "new town" from the 1960s; a circular stone platform surrounding a water well into which South Asian women are dipping buckets; a round navigation radar screen; a busy traffic roundabout; the loop formed by a red grosgrain AIDS-awareness lapel pin; a cat's eye; dozens of people standing in a field forming a huge peace symbol when viewed from above; the sun beginning to reappear from behind the moon after a solar eclipse (see Figure 3.2). Sleekly elegant in its simplicity, the brochure uses text sparingly to tell the Forum's story, concluding with a final section on "world class governance:" "we are striving towards a world-class corporate governance system where values are as important a basis as rules."[13]

As is clear from the carefully crafted mission statements, discursive tags and visuals, Forum officials construct the identity of the Forum as important, useful, boundary-crossing, socially beneficial and unique. The Forum staff need to be able to explain these identity attributes, both to themselves and to others. Among other reasons, it forms the core of the rationale for the key marketing and community relations functions. To explain the Forum's identity attributes requires the generation of an evolutionary narrative to account for how it came to be as it is today: a creation myth, as it were. Staff who join the Forum today need to learn it and understand the story, even if unconsciously and passively, in order to do their new jobs well and to be able to communicate about the Forum effectively to outsiders. Meeting managing directors and other senior staff today, one can see just how effective the Forum has been as transmitting its evolutionary narrative: senior managers who have worked for the Forum for only a few years are able to communicate the history and objectives of the Forum using the same language as Klaus Schwab. They stay on-message. Schwab's role in steering the Forum since its inception and meeting challenges as they have arisen has been a major part of the transmission of the Forum's evolutionary narrative and construction of its internal identity. This makes the current period all the more important in terms of preparation for Schwab's retirement and succession, as evidenced by plans for creation of a university degree programme specifically to train global leaders, and by extension Forum leaders (see Chapter 7). The Forum staff alone, however, do not bear exclusive responsibility

Figure 3.2 Two of a series of images from the World Economic Forum's 2005 promotional brochure illustrating the repetition of the Forum's globe motif

for generating and recounting an internal identity narrative: the Forum's members must be understood as key components of the project as well. Member firms of the Forum of necessity must buy into a significant portion of the Forum's own identity narrative, or else they would not find membership attractive and cost-effective: in order to be attractive to members, the Forum must do what its says it does, and it must do it well. The percentage of member firms that have been members of the Forum for over ten years, 28 percent, is a strong indicator of how much firms participate in the Forum's identity narrative.

The internal evolutionary narrative that has been generated by the Forum has focused on the expansion of cooperation amongst global stakeholders, the institution's readiness to adapt rapidly to political and economic change, and the adoption of cutting-edge technologies to serve members and disseminate information to global constituencies. Schwab's use of the notion of milestones to demarcate the growth and development of the Forum's scope and mission paints the Forum narrative as one of progression from ambitious beginnings, but often in terms of quick response to external political and economic changes, such as the Yom Kippur War and Arab oil embargo, the end of the Cold War, or the attacks of 11 September 2001. Although there appears to be no immanent teleology, no grand design mapping the road from Davos 1971 to Davos 2006, clearly the Forum's own narrative is one of expanding its mission and its scope. What will constitute the natural or ideal extent of the Forum's future size and range of activities is far from certain, but it is clear that the Forum today sees itself as nowhere near that point yet.

4 Generating knowledge today

World Economic Forum meetings in 2005

Introduction: different narratives of two summits

This chapter explores two of the major meetings of the World Economic Forum in 2005: the Davos Annual Meeting at the end of January and the India Economic Summit in New Delhi at the end of November. Although the two events were of different orders of importance in terms of the Forum's annual agenda, the narrative of each event contributes crucial elements to an understanding of the Forum's most public activities. Davos remains the signature conference of the Forum each year, attracting the highest level and most illustrious list of attendees, whilst New Delhi was one of several annual regional summits. However, the two meetings are similar in terms of structure and format. Taken together they span the year in the public life of the Forum. The India Economic Summit is arguably the most important of the Forum's regional meetings, given the Forum's historical relationship with India and the CII (see Chapter 1). Also, as the last event before the 2006 Davos meeting, the Delhi meeting was perceived as of particular importance in 2005 in light of the Forum's increasing concentration upon India's "growth and democracy" model and China's growing role in the global political economy. The two narratives with accompanying analysis seek to bring greater depth of understanding of the core of the Forum: the interaction between members and between members and guests at Forum events. Two different narrative approaches are taken in order to give different perspectives on Forum meetings. The 2005 Annual Meeting at Davos is reviewed from several external perspectives, including a collation of the public record of the highlights of the meeting, an account of the Forum's narrative of the meeting and a review of how the media covered the meeting. By contrast, the narrative of the India Economic Summit is told experientially from the perspective of the author as an invited guest. The narrative recounts experiences of panels and other meeting sessions, as well as social occasions and the individuals who attended. Both narratives seek to convey the importance of the Forum's construction of the visual, aesthetic and experiential quality of Forum events for participants. Neither narrative approach can claim to be comprehensive, but taken together they contribute to building a composite, layered understanding of the personalities and interactions that make Forum meetings the knowledge-generating and information-exchanging events that they are.

The 2005 Davos Annual Meeting: "Taking Responsibility for Tough Choices"

Introduction to Davos: a global town hall

Titled "Taking Responsibility for Tough Choices," the 2005 Annual Meeting at Davos gave the impression of reaching a new level, not only in terms of what the Forum had been doing all along, but even to the extent of accelerating the expansion of the Forum's own claim on a global mandate for its mission. To an extent never before seen, the themes and subjects of the 2005 Davos panels, roundtables, speeches and discussions seemed to embrace, lay claim to, and, in the Forum's own idiom, "take responsibility for," the development of global values, norms and ethics. As if to assert this global mandate boldly right from the start, on the first day of the summit the Forum staged its first ever "Global Town Hall" meeting, a three-hour session in which around 700 of the summit's 2,250 participants from ninety-six countries debated and were polled electronically on which values should underpin global governance and which issues should be the most important global priorities going forward (see Figure 4.1). As ever, the Forum made extensive use of the most up-to-date information technology to facilitate the Global Town Hall, to gather information about the demographic breakdown of the attendees (see Figure 4.2), to assess what were their major issues of global concern, and to bring their collective views into the discussion in real time.

Town Hall participants were organized into "facilitated, technology-enabled discussions" around tables of ten. Information about the content and conclusions of each table's deliberations was tabulated, processed, synthesized and displayed electronically for the entire gathering to digest. Participants then voted electronically using handheld devices to select six global priorities for discussion out of a possible pre-selected twelve, plus two additional priorities identified by

Figure 4.1 The Global Town Hall meeting at the World Economic Forum's 2005 Annual Meeting, Davos, Switzerland

the delegates themselves, and to identify key challenges within each of their six chosen priority areas.[1] The results served to validate the summit's agenda and set the tone for the rest of the panels and discussions.

The data suggest that the majority of the conference's participants remained early middle-aged male North American and European businesspeople.[2] Yet although the demographic distribution of participants may not have been reflective of global civil society, the preponderance of the subjects discussed by those attending the Town Hall, which included 23 heads of state, 72 cabinet-level ministers, 26 religious leaders, 50 heads of CSOs, 15 trades union leaders, and nearly 500 leaders of global businesses, did not reflect the same issue priorities as such a gathering of male Euro-American business leaders might have reflected even ten years earlier.[3]

The overarching theme of the Davos 2005 discussions, and the representations to the global public thereof, centred on global social concerns: alleviation of poverty, particularly in Africa; aid for victims of natural and other disasters, brought sharply into focus by the Indonesian earthquake and Indian Ocean tsunami of 26 December 2004, which killed over 250,000 people; corporate social responsibility; and inclusiveness, in the sense of undertaking the Davos discussions

WHO TOOK PART IN THE GLOBAL TOWN HALL

	Town Hall Participants	World Comparison
Gender		
Male	66%	50.3%
Female	34%	49.7%
Age		
Younger than 20	0%	37%
20-29	1%	17%
30-39	11%	15%
40-49	28%	12%
50-59	41%	9%
60-69	16%	6%
70-79	3%	3%
80 or older	1%	1%
Region of Residence		
Asia-Pacific	15%	57%
Africa	4%	13%
Europe	35%	13%
Latin America	4%	9%
Middle East	8%	3%
North America	35%	5%
Profession		
Academia	9%	NA
Business	50%	NA
NGO	8%	NA
Government	6%	NA
Media	9%	NA
Religion	1%	NA
Arts	3%	NA
Science & Medicine	4%	NA
Other	10%	NA

Figure 4.2 Demographic breakdown of attendees at the Davos Global Town Hall meeting, January 2005

Source: World Economic Forum 2005, 'Annual Meeting 2005, Davos, Switzerland; Taking Responsibility for Tough Choices'.

with a broad cross-section of global civil society represented. Forum organizers constructed the discussions to be conducted explicitly in an ethical space: in the domain of values. At the Global Town Hall, even before debating and choosing global priorities for discussion, participants were invited to discuss what values they thought should steer global leaders in their decisionmaking processes. Participants' most favoured values were integrity, compassion, equity, tolerance, selflessness and stewardship. Bearing these values in mind, the delegates were asked to select six global priorities for discussion. They chose the following, in order by percentage of participants voting for each issue as one of their six choices:

Poverty	64.4 percent
Equitable globalization	54.9 percent
Climate change	51.2 percent
Education	43.9 percent
The Middle East	43.7 percent
Global governance	43.2 percent.[4]

The approach to the global priority issues, as revealed by the challenges that the Global Town Hall participants identified for each, is hard to differentiate from that of CSOs that focus on development aid. Important challenges identified in overcoming poverty, for example, include the need for the developed world to fund infrastructure and access to markets, and for leaders to think more globally. Developing countries, by contrast, need to promote greater transparency in government, education, healthcare and gender equity, and need to be more willing to help themselves.

As with other recent Davos meetings, there were three distinct public information streams for the rest of the world to interpret: the content of the events themselves, which can be interpreted through transcripts, interviews and other direct observations; the Forum's own representation of the events, available to the general public through the Forum website, audio and video clips provided to the media; and the media's own representation of the summit, based on on-site reportage and Forum information feeds. Behind and beyond these public information streams lies a private body of information and knowledge accumulated and shared between Forum members that is not available for viewing or interpretation directly by the public, but can only be interpreted secondarily through analysis of public initiatives, business deals, and other projects likely to follow on from the summit. The review of the three public information streams, which follows, nonetheless creates a useful set of images of Davos that shed light on both the processes and products of a Forum Annual Meeting.

The events of Davos: fighting poverty and growing markets

Each Annual Meeting is co-chaired by a team of marquee names from global business, usually CEOs of firms who have signed up to be Annual Meeting Partners of the Forum for a given year. For the Forum's management, the leaders of a Davos summit play an important role in communicating the ethos of the gathering to the participants and to the outside world. The co-chairs of the summit were the even more public face of Davos, itself the most public face of the World Economic Forum. The 2005 summit was co-chaired by six senior executives representing diversity across a spectrum of regions, types of business and genders, as indicated by the format in which they were listed on the Forum website:

- Bill Gates, co-founder, Bill and Melinda Gates Foundation, and Chairman and Chief Software Architect, Microsoft Corporation, USA.
- N. R. Narayana Murthy, Chairman of the Board and Chief Mentor, Infosys Technologies, India.
- Lubna S. Olayan, Chief Executive Officer, Olayan Financing Company, Saudi Arabia.
- Charles Prince, Chief Executive Officer, Citigroup, USA.
  John A. Thain, Chief Executive Officer, New York Stock Exchange, USA.
- Daniel Vasella, Chairman and Chief Executive Officer, Novartis, Switzerland.

Notwithstanding the preponderance of male Americans and leaders of technology and financial businesses, within this small group women, the Arab world and the emerging Asian Great Powers had high visibility. Lubna Olayan is a leading Saudi financier. One of only a small number of women CEOs of major Middle Eastern firms, Olayan is CEO of Olayan Financing, a firm with over $2 billion in assets, $1 billion in sales and over 8800 employees in 2001.[5] Ranked by *Fortune* Magazine as one of the fifty most powerful women outside of the United States, Olayan has spoken out aggressively in Saudi Arabia in favour of gender equality as part of a strategy for Saudi economic growth.[6] N. R. Narayana Murthy is Chairman of one of India's largest firms, Infosys, which is a leader in global technology.

So what "happened" over the five days of Davos 2005, beyond the 200-plus panel discussions and plenary sessions, social events and countless public and private meetings between the attendees? For the Forum's management, the challenge is to tell a story to the public that conveys the impression of a link between thought and action, between Davos discussions and real-world results. For the media, the challenge is to interpret the Forum's own narrative of Davos and to find stories of their own that inform, and entertain, their audience, and in so doing to sell copy. Hence for the media, the events of Davos tend to conflate into stories about mood and general sentiments running through the panels and vignettes about particular meetings, dinners and celebrities (see below). However, one of the most significant features of Davos as a venue for public discourse is the opportunity it affords for fore-grounding social, economic and political issues through its unique channels of communication on the global stage. Participants did this in various ways. The most obvious and visible of these ways is the sched-uled, "headline" speech, which is a featured part of the official program, and which can be interpreted on its own merits irrespective of media "spin" or Forum publicity.

At Davos 2005, perhaps the best example of a headline speech was British Prime Minister Tony Blair's address to the opening plenary session of the summit on 27 January 2005, which he organized around the theme of global "interdependence." Blair's contention was that, whilst the global chain of events following 9/11 had caused the world's problems and divisions to stand out in sharper relief, the same events had also underscored the reality of interdependence and the need for cooperation in global problemsolving. In this vein Blair used his speech to attempt to "sell" US President George W. Bush's inaugural address of the previous week to the assemblage at Davos representing the global community. Blair contended that Bush's speech in Washington indicated an evolution of US foreign policy toward a more cooperative approach, recognizing the necessity of interdepen-dence for solving key global problems such as poverty and terrorism..As Blair saw it, the shift in the US approach opened the way for a common global effort to address five key problems: fighting terrorism through democratization, supporting transformation in Iraq, solving the Israeli-Palestinian conflict, addressing global climate change and ending poverty in Africa. Highlighting the latter two items as the core of Britain's presidency of the G8, Blair pressed for support for Britain's proposed solutions: among other things, a doubling of Africa aid through mechanisms such as an International Finance Facility and a major increase in conflict resolution efforts. On climate control Blair stated his willingness to accept the Bush administration's refusal to sign the Kyoto protocol and commit to its methods and timelines for greenhouse gas reductions, provided the United States accepted the necessity of achieving its objectives and worked with his G8 initiatives for industrial and developing countries alike.[7] Blair's address was tactically well thought out, in that it took advantage of an audience of arguably the highest-profile cross-section of global business and civil society to build support for major global governance initiatives that were likely to face substantial political opposition. By doing so at Davos, in the process he also validated the Forum's claims for the preeminence of the Annual Meeting and the consequent expectations of its attendees.

A global platform for policy debate

Another approach that many political and business leaders took to raise the profile of social, economic and political issues was to use Davos as a platform to speak out publicly through the media on major policy debates underway at home or in global arenas. This strategy effectively capitalizes on the global media attention focused on the Davos "stage" to capture more coverage, better story placement and a more arresting visual backdrop for their story. US Senator Richard Shelby (Republican-Alabama), chairman of the Senate Banking Committee, articulated concerns about the prospects for passing social security reform legislation sought by President Bush, while Senator John McCain (Republican-Arizona), a former US presidential candidate, expressed greater optimism, provided Bush was able to win some support from Congressional Democrats.[8] Pakistani Prime Minister Shaukat Aziz revealed in an interview at Davos that the following week he would propose to India's Prime Minister Manmohan Singh a new set of bilateral confidence-building measures without prejudicing the resolution of their dispute over Kashmir.[9] Aziz also took advantage of the attention from global business leaders at Davos to market the Pakistani government's economic reform program, including the planned privatizations of all Pakistani state-owned firms, and the recent successes of Pakistan's economy, with 2004 growth reported at 6.4 percent and 2005 growth of 7 percent targeted.[10] George Soros, the largest donor to the campaign to defeat George W. Bush's US presidential re-election bid, used an interview at Davos with Bloomberg Media to argue that Democratic presidential challenger Senator John Kerry had failed to articulate a credible economic alternative that would resonate with voters.[11]

Perhaps the most significant global public policy debate that played on the media stage at Davos concerned US public finances and their impact on the relative value of the US dollar. Microsoft chairman Bill Gates used an interview with Charlie Rose of the US network PBS to discuss the US dollar, predicting its value would fall because of unprecedented levels of US government debt, echoing criticism of the US federal budget deficit made the previous day at Davos by German Deputy Finance Minister Caio Koch-Weser. The debate at Davos over US public finances raged on, with Yu Yongding, an adviser to China's central bank, calling on Washington to lower the US current account deficit and stop pressing China to revalue the yuan, even as he suggested the time was right for China to revalue. Yu's comments prompted a Chinese central bank official in Beijing to comment anonymously that Yu's opinions were his own and that China remained committed to the yuan's fixed peg against the US dollar.[12]

Davos 2005 lived up to its promise to advance global debate on new solutions to ending poverty when France's President Jacques Chirac publicly proposed creating a new global tax, such as a duty on aviation fuel, financial transactions or capital flows, to fund development aid. Chirac succeeded in engaging the summit's major participants in the central theme of how best to fight poverty. Speaking at a Davos panel discussion, South Africa's President Thabo Mbeki expressed concern that such a tax would be too difficult and too time consuming to be enacted by the world's parliaments and would thus distract attention from more effective means of increasing development aid. Bill Clinton echoed Mbeki's concern, doubting that a global tax proposal would garner sufficient global political backing to be enacted. Bill Gates speculated that it would take 5–10 years for a global tax to be enacted. Tony Blair, by contrast, advocated keeping the proposal on the table, while Bono pressed for total debt forgiveness by the IMF and World Bank of the debts of the poorest countries as a more effective mechanism.[13]

A more philosophical debate about the nature of capitalism, which was close to the centre of the discursive focus of Davos 2005, was entered by Lord Browne, chairman of BP. Lord Browne criticized the spread of what he called "pseudo markets" within government institutions responsible for the delivery of public services. Browne said the implementation of market mechanisms in institutions such as universities, prisons and hospitals was "damaging the professional ethos" in public bodies. In Lord Browne's view, for government to deploy market-like mechanisms in the delivery of core public services risked heightening negative public sentiment toward the private sector more broadly. Browne's comments were reported in the media in the context of a political debate in Britain pitting Tony Blair's plans to use market mechanisms to improve efficiency in public services delivery against the skepticism of Chancellor of the Exchequer (and Labour Party sometime political rival) Gordon Brown toward such plans.[14] However, the broader issue has been on the political agenda in most developed and developing countries alike. Lord Browne's concerns were indicative of how business leaders have become more sensitive to how the public perceive the structuring of markets through political bargaining and to how public attitudes to business may shift as a result of how markets are structured.

A Davos Annual Meeting also serves as an ideal venue for using public diplomacy to advance ongoing multilateral cooperative projects, such as the World Trade Organization's Doha Development Round of trade liberalization negotiations. Then-WTO Director General Supachai Panitchpakdi spoke publicly at Davos to urge WTO member countries to redouble their efforts and to make commitments by summer 2005 that would lead to a successful conclusion of the trade round. With a WTO ministerial meeting to agree a draft trade agreement already scheduled for Hong Kong in December 2005, much remained to be done to close the huge gaps remaining in major member countries' positions, especially on subsidies and agricultural trade.[15] As Panitchpakdi was scheduled to meet with trade ministers of twenty WTO member countries on the final day of the conference, to speak out at the beginning was tactically astute, as it set the stage for interchange between government, business and civil society officials in the panel discussions to build diplomatic momentum favouring the making of concessions to complete the round.

The summit according to the Forum: "the spirit of Davos"

The Forum's website was richer in detail, content and color than ever, even if by the same token more carefully content-managed than in previous years. On the site the summit featured a full representation of global civil society, expressing a full range of often controversial views on most of the important contemporary world issues. The online images and text seemed to proclaim that no longer could Davos be said to be a close-knit gathering of clever brains drawn primarily from business, with a short list of invited interlocutors, brainstorming about global problems in an intimate setting. The Forum's representation of the participants at Davos in January 2005 was a claim on global legitimacy: an assertion or presumption that the gathered assemblage was qualified and

empowered to deliberate on and seek resolution of crucial world problems, ranging from poverty in Africa and violence in the Middle East
to macroeconomic policy weakness in the United States and flawed
structures of global corporate governance. The Forum had taken its
public diplomacy up a notch from its already high standard.

The challenge for Forum public relations and public diplomacy was
how to convey an audiovisually rich image of the Davos meeting that
left the viewer at the end with a positive feeling about Davos and about
the Forum in general. An eight-minute video, "The Spirit of Davos,"
which viewers of the Forum website could view during and after Davos
2005, achieved this objective well by constructing carefully, beautifully
and dramatically for the web-accessible global public the Forum's
conception of the Annual Meeting's role and importance. The video
began and ended with dramatic footage of Earth viewed from the
international space station, which created a sense of gravitas regarding
the mission of the summit and framed visually for viewers the Forum's
claim of global legitimacy for the summit's objectives. The opening
sequence cut to picturesque visuals of snow-covered Davos and the
surrounding Swiss countryside and music appropriate to reinforce the
ambience, supplied shots of famous world political leaders arriving at
Davos, and culminated with Klaus Schwab making a defining statement about the summit: "the spirit of Davos is the spirit of dialogue
and cooperation, not confrontation."16 There then followed a montage
of clips from the 2004 Davos summit, emphasizing the themes of
content and method that the Forum was seeking to transmit to the
public. The montage began with Jose Maria Figueres, then CEO of the
World Economic Forum, emphasizing the Forum's concentration on
the post-9/11 link between security and economic growth. Stating that
"prosperity and security are two sides of the same coin," Figueres
called for action on both issues. Later in the video Mozambican president Joacquim Chissano would echo the sentiment, arguing that peace
is necessary to build prosperity. Figueres also underlined the importance of partnership, a key Forum theme: "partnering is the name of
the game."17 Immediately following Figueres, former US President Bill
Clinton commented on the importance of the Davos participants
learning from one another about how to make a greater impact on the
issues about which they are most concerned. After Clinton appeared,
there were soundbites from a range of corporate leaders, such as then-
CEO of Hewlett Packard, Carly Fiorina, carefully interspersed with
those of political leaders, such as Nigerian President Olusegun
Obasanjo, British Foreign Secretary Jack Straw and Egyptian Foreign
Minister Amr Moussa, and leaders of civil society organizations, such

as Irene Khan of Amnesty International and Bali Namrata of the Self-employed Women's Association of India. Addressing topics ranging from corporate social responsibility to democratization to terrorism, their effect was to convey a sense that the major topics of world concern were being discussed at Davos by a full ensemble of global leadership representing North and South, East and West, male and female, and other relevant cleavages of culture.

As the video drew to a close, the theme shifted from soundbites on issues of concern to praise for the Forum itself. John Chambers, CEO of Cisco Systems, praised the Forum for creating a unique venue for dialogue and amassing resources for good. His sentiments were echoed by then-World Bank President James Wolfensohn. Shots of Bill Clinton hugging people were followed by UN Secretary-General Kofi Annan lauding the Forum for taking leadership in creating "public values as well as private profit." Annan's endorsement communicated an imprimatur of global public support, in the voice of the United Nations, for the Forum's ongoing public and private roles. The video reached its climactic conclusion with what was intended to be the most visually arresting footage, earthrise viewed from the international space station. British NASA astronaut Michael Foale and Russian cosmonaut Alexandr Kalery, who were staffing the space station at the time, delivered a message that viewers of the video were told was broadcast to the summit participants at Davos. Foale constructs for viewers an image of globality coupled with environmental responsibility: "As we work on the International Space Station, we witness daily the beauty, the fragility of our planet Earth. From our own unique vantage point we can barely see borders or territories." Then with serious and earnest, yet nonetheless cheerful, demeanour, the two spacemen exhorted the Davos participants to do their best to achieve their global mission: "We encourage your members to actively participate [*sic*] in this World Economic Forum, as you strive to find the solutions required to improve the lives of all Earth's citizens."[18] The final shot shows Earth as seen from the space station, but, interestingly, the portion of Earth shown is only ocean, with no land masses visible. The Earth view then fades to a scene of Davos under snow and the video ends. The video appeared to have achieved its objective of leaving the visitor to the website with warm feelings about the Forum and the Annual Meeting participants, and a sense of the importance and seriousness of the Davos mission.[19]

Moving from the spirit to the substance of Davos 2005 on video, content on the Forum site is reasonably rich and meaty. Viewers can watch full webcasts of the major plenary speeches of the conference, including those by Tony Blair, Chinese Vice Premier Huang Ju, European Commission President Jose Manuel Barroso, and Ukrainian President Victor Yushchenko, and substantial digests of the Global Town Hall meeting, and key panel discussions on, among other things, US foreign policy, prospects for the global economy in 2005, debt relief for Africa, fighting corporate corruption, and the Middle East peace process. On the website the viewer can also find text summaries of each of the 200-plus panel discussions, a vast offering that, for the reader with the time and inclination to review it all, provides a very comprehensive survey of what the participants at Davos actually spent most of their time thinking about and discussing. Each summary is a concise (approximately one page of text) précis of what was discussed, including major interventions by panelists. For example, at a panel discussion on "The Economics of Populism" held on 27 January, panelists began by discussing what the term "populism" means. Disagreement between panelists was recorded, not only about what populism is, but also regarding its effects. Mario Blejer, an adviser to the Governor of the Bank of England, argued that populism had been killed by globalization. Because they are inconsistent with neoliberal macroeconomic norms and constraints, the distributional and growth policies favoured by populists ended up making their constituents worse of instead of better. Theodore Zeldin of the Oxford Muse contested this view, arguing that populism retains its appeal because it is emotionally driven by the frustration of individuals when confronted with perceived inequalities. Neoliberal development scholar Hernando de Soto, president of the Instituto Libertad y Democracia in Lima, contended that contemporary populism had a choice between making a liberal market economy more accessible to the majority of the population or else abandoning a market economy altogether. The summaries of the panel discussions tend not to indicate that the panels drew any clear conclusions from their discussions. Rather, they give the flavour that the function of the panels was to draw out for those attending (and, in a more derivative way, for those reading the summaries) the nature of the issues to be debated, the major points of view, and at least the beginnings of the main arguments between them. Given that the duration of the panels makes this probably the most that is practicable, the website's précis of each panel appears to achieve its objective for the reader in equal measure. A visitor to the website unfamiliar with the issue of populism, for example, can familiarize herself quickly with some of the main questions and disagreements regarding populism's definitions and effects as perceived by a range of panelists from, ideally, different geographical, professional and political backgrounds.

The summit according to the media

As in past years, media coverage of Davos 2005 ranged from reportage of the substance of the panels and other meetings to "lifestyle" pieces focusing on the activities of celebrities and the ambience of the summit: what it is like to attend a major world event that is not open to the public.

> In a world full of mediocre conferences, Davos is the one not to miss. It is the granddaddy of all networking events, where the big boys turn out. A place where [Dell CEO Michael] Dell comes to learn more about running a company.[20]

Beyond the feature articles and TV spots focusing on Richard Gere's speech on HIV/AIDS or Sharon Stone raising $1 million at a Davos seminar to fight malaria in Tanzania,[21] some journalists produced articles that concentrated on the contested aspects of Davos and the Forum itself, as well as reflecting on the role of the media at Davos and in representing Davos to the outside world. BBC News website business editor Tim Weber highlighted debate over the value of having pop music and film stars in attendance, noting that some Davos participants criticized celebrities for being ersatz cultural leaders, whilst others praised their ability to focus the attention of business attendees on fighting poverty. Weber also focused on the importance of the summit for politicians from across the globe to communicate with US officials, noting general displeasure that the only senior US government official in attendance was outgoing US Trade Representative/incoming Deputy Secretary of State Robert Zoellick. This resulted in US Senate Majority Leader Bill Frist (R.-Tennessee) and Senator John McCain (R.-Arizona), the most influential of nine US senators in attendance, having to serve as primary interlocutors for those seeking change in Bush administration foreign policy.[22] Weber also documented the importance of Davos for members of the Forum to network. Networking possibilities benefited the summit's invited guests too, Weber observed, citing the enthusiasm of Benjamin Zander, conductor of the Boston Philharmonic Orchestra, for invitations he received at Davos to make visits and give speeches. Praising the mix of cultures and backgrounds of Davos participants for their ability to open the mind, Zander said of the summit: "This is thought globalization."[23]

In an in-depth article in the *New York Times*, Timothy O'Brien panned the celebrity hype that attracts the bulk of non-business media attention and assessed the value of the summit to its participants.

O'Brien quoted Schwab's justification for the summit, which referenced the essential multi-stakeholder mission of the Forum: "If we didn't exist, someone would have to create us. . . . Global challenges are not solved by business alone, by not-for-profits alone. They are solved by collaboration, and it requires a multi-stakeholder platform."[24] In his interview with O'Brien, Schwab called Davos "a mirror of the global agenda."

O'Brien's article focused on the character of the relationships between the Davos participants. Infosys Chairman N. R. Narayana Murthy, one of the chairs of Davos 2005, invoked the British sociological notion of "clubability" to characterize the Davos discourse, likening it to a saying at Infosys: "you can disagree with me as long as you're not disagreeable." For Narayana Murthy, this is the spirit of Davos: "if you are open-minded you listen to others, and if you listen to others you become more open-minded."[25] O'Brien also mentioned the main criticisms of Davos: that made by non-attendees, that the summit's public social-political agenda is a screen for private networking and dealmaking; and that made by long-time attendees, that the summit has become too big, scheduled and staid. O'Brien went on to highlight the notion of "Davos man," a sociological descriptor of attendees of Davos popularized by Samuel Huntington in a 1993 essay in which Huntington castigated the wealthy, educated Western elites who attended Davos for being insulated from external threats to their world and the populations from which those threats emerge. But according to O'Brien, Davos man is a generalization that can be broken down: Schwab himself commented that 50 percent of the corporate membership was actively committed to the Forum's social goals, 30 percent were members primarily to attend Davos, and the remaining 20 percent were "followers" who were members primarily to benefit from the networking opportunities.

Journalist and scholar Timothy Garton Ash, writing in the *Guardian*, also criticized the notion of Davos man as a globalized cadre of white, Western, middle-aged male elites. Garton Ash found the rhetoric of Davos 2005 participants to be more polarized between European and American perspectives than at previous summits, and was troubled by the increasing lack of communication and understanding between the two sides of the Atlantic, especially given that, national origin notwithstanding, Davos attendees still have amongst the most cosmopolitan mindsets of those on their respective continents. Were this ongoing deterioration of transatlantic political relations evident at Davos 2005, despite ever increasing economic interdependence, to continue, Garton Ash foresaw it as advancing the prospect of rising

Asian economies eclipsing the historical dominance of Europe and North America, with unforeseeable consequences resulting.[26]

Sunday Times economics editor David Smith concentrated on the opportunity Davos presented to UK Chancellor of the Exchequer Gordon Brown to advance his own agenda for raising $50 billion over ten years for fighting poverty in Africa through a special bond issue. Brown's Davos diary was packed: he appeared on a panel with Bono, Bill Gates and Brazilian President Ignacio Lula da Silva, gave a luncheon for journalists, met with British business leaders, and gave three press conferences. Interviewed by Smith at Davos, Brown was enthusiastic about having obtained the backing of German Chancellor Gerhard Schröder for his aid scheme. Smith's interview with Brown was cut short by the arrival of Bono, a major supporter of Brown, for a "bilateral" meeting. Telling Smith the feeling was mutual, Brown averred that real political power lies with rock stars.[27]

Going beyond feature coverage of the conference and its issues, probably the most important role that the media play at Davos is to serve as the communication channel for attendees wishing to communicate to the global public. This applies not just to foreign ministers, presidents and secretaries-general. When leaders of an industry sector want to address emerging issues of concern and to engage in public diplomacy designed to persuade a broader cross-section of business and political opinion to share their own perspective, Davos provides an ideal venue, in large part because it has the full attention of the global business media. For example, hedge fund managers used Davos 2005 to launch a campaign to head off growing sentiments in the United States and Europe that hedge funds need to be regulated. Mindful of investor fears that hedge fund investing had taken on some of the characteristics of a bubble, having grown from $50 billion to $1 trillion in assets under management in fifteen years, the US Securities and Exchange Commission required hedge funds to register with the SEC, and their European regulatory counterparts have been contemplating following suit. Hedge funds do not need to be regulated, fund managers argued, because by betting against prevailing sentiment they reduce the volatility of markets rather than increasing it.[28]

The 2005 India Economic Summit: a participant's view

Unlike the overlapping narratives of Davos, this narrative of the Forum's 2005 India Economic Summit, which took place on 27–29 November in New Delhi, is recounted from the perspective of the author's personal observations as an attendee. For participants, the

2005 India Economic Summit in New Delhi began a few weeks before the meeting actually convened, when the Forum sent out to each a password permitting access to the members' and participants' area of the Forum website and an invitation to view in advance a detailed programme of the summit agenda and to take advantage of the Forum's "Knowledge Concierge" service, which allows viewers to download short digests of issues and topics to be discussed at meetings. The private content on the website is not that deep, but it does allow attendees to plan ahead for whom they want to contact, which panels they wish to attend and upon which particular issues they may wish to focus. Upon arrival in Delhi at the conference hotel, the comfortable and contemporary Taj Palace, for the start of the summit, the Forum's formidable organizational skills are most visible in their very lack of intrusiveness. At the dedicated registration kiosks, at which the 750–800 attendees are issued their pre-prepared digitally barcoded photo ID badges and packets containing official programs, the all-important facebooks, and other logistical information, the atmosphere is relaxed, friendly and welcoming. Descending the escalator to the conference level, along one side of the corridor leading to the conference rooms a bank of terminals sat waiting for participants using their ID barcodes, to send and retrieve summit-related emails sent through an internal Forum network or to access the internet. Nearby was a well provisioned media resource room. Immediately outside of the two main conference rooms was a documentation centre with numerous brochures and booklets about programs of the Forum and co-hosts the Confederation of Indian Industry (CII); summaries of the panel and plenary sessions as they were completed; and information about partner firms of the Forum. In contrast to many meetings of international organizations, security throughout the summit was so discreet as to be all but invisible. This changed only on the afternoon of Indian Prime Minister Manmohan Singh's address to the closing plenary session, when hotel entrances were closed, metal detectors deployed and searches of bags implemented. The overall relaxed face to security without doubt contributed to the intimate, club-like atmosphere of the group gathered in Delhi for three days to meet and converse.

The Forum's Delhi programme was truly demanding, at least for those participants intending to get the most out of it. The summit began on Sunday 27 November with a plenary session in the late morning and continued over three days packed with events, from breakfast through until late evening entertainment and cultural programs, until a reception late in the afternoon of Tuesday 29 November brought the proceedings to a close. Mornings and afternoons were filled with panel discussions, from which there were usually two or three choices in each time slot, punctuated occasionally by plenary sessions on sufficiently central topics or with sufficiently important speakers that everyone was expected to attend. Mealtimes were not excluded from the packed agenda. Monday morning the 28th began with a 7.45 a.m. "working breakfast" on foreign direct investment in India. Luncheons were also all about the business of the summit, but business that was social by nature as well. On Sunday the 27th, for what was billed in the programme as a "networking lunch," an extensive buffet was served on one of the terraces in the Taj Palace Hotel's extensive gardens. Attendees were free to seat themselves at round tables to eat, meet old friends and acquaintances and introduce themselves to new ones. This was the first opportunity for attendees to have a good look at whom else was attending: a range of participants extending from CEOs and senior executives of Forum member firms to members of the Confederation of Indian Industry, the Forum's host partner for the summit of twenty years, to European and Asian media and academics and members of the Forum for Young Global Leaders. Social entrepreneurs, affiliated with the Schwab Foundation for Social Entrepreneurship, were very much in evidence, with participants ranging from Sadhguru Jaggi Vasudev, founder of the Isha Foundation, an Indian not-for-profit foundation teaching inner well-being through yoga, to Safia Minney, founder of People Tree, a fair trade and ecological fashion and handicrafts company operating in Britain and Japan. As was the case with virtually all of the events of the summit, seating was open: one could find oneself sitting at a table with one of the Forum's managing directors, a CEO of one of India's largest firms or a senior government official from the Indian Government or the European Union. And so the first of many rounds of meetings, exchanges of ubiquitous business cards, and planting the seeds of future networks of contacts, began. Luncheons on subsequent days were more structured. Billed as "working lunches," they were in fact panel or speaker sessions at which the hotel served lunch to participants during the proceedings. Dinners were occasions for culture and commerce, as will be discussed below.

At the plenaries and panel sessions, and at the social gatherings as well, the focus of the 2005 India Economic Summit was on the rise of India in the global economy. At this summit India was the star, and a star of Bollywood/Hollywood proportions. The feeling that India, long thought of in the West as a "developing country," had become a major player in the global economy and a "great power" politically ran throughout all the sessions. Whilst building for several years, with India's economy growing at close to 8 percent per annum, the buzz and excitement shared by a large number of the participants about India's accomplishments and its future prospects was palpable. The first working session on Sunday morning framed this dominant discourse of India's achievements and future policy choices by exploring three broad-brush scenarios of India's possible political, economic and social development over the coming twenty years and the different combinations of external circumstances and policy choices that might make each scenario a reality. Entitled "India and the World: Scenarios to 2025," the session showcased scenario building, one of the more recent major directions in which the Forum has been developing its research capacity recently. Under the direction of the Forum's Centre for Strategic Insight, research is commissioned that maps possible sets of policy choices by government, business and civil society against possible sets of external economic, political and social conditions, and generates a small number of scenarios showing how those mappings might produce future economic, political and social conditions. The objective of presenting the scenarios is to get business, government and civil society leaders to internalize the understanding that just as external constraints do not determine domestic policies, likewise policy choices are not made in a vacuum and do have consequences through their impact upon and reaction with global affairs. Presenting three contrasting scenarios of India's future development right at the beginning of the summit played an important agenda-setting role for the rest of the sessions by encouraging participants to discuss ideas and policy options raised in these discursive terms (Figure 4.3).

The scenario session featured a high-level roster of presenters, with an introduction by Ged Davis, the Forum Managing Director who chairs the Centre for Strategic Insight, and N. Srinivasan, the Director-General of the CII, in the chair. Each scenario was presented by a different luminary from the Indian business community. The first scenario, dubbed Bolly World, was presented by Malvinder Singh, President, Pharmaceuticals, of one of India's most successful, high-flying biotechnology companies, Ranbaxy Laboratories, and also one of the Forum's Young Global Leaders. Under the Bolly World scenario, the middle of the three possibilities, India's productivity and wages approach world levels by 2015, giving the impression of successful growth, but the rest of the economy does not keep up. Complacency sets in about the importance of reforms to infrastructure, education and developing public-private partnerships. After 2015, although poverty has declined from 25 percent to 17 percent of the population, rural areas lag behind, and rising social tensions and political strife result. Growth slows, new more aggressive forms of political

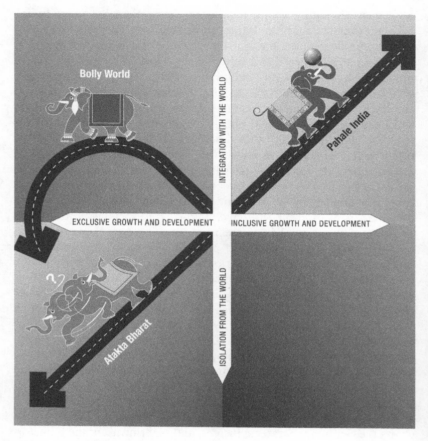

Figure 4.3 Graphic illustrating three scenarios of India's possible economic growth, articulated in terms of Bollywood film-style plot narratives

Source: World Economic Forum 2005, 'India and the World: Scenarios to 2025, Executive Summary'.

representation emerge, foreign investors become disillusioned and foreign direct investment in India declines. Thus spurned by her new global friends, India turns back toward her older group of friends amongst less developed countries, who are not keen to take India back into the fold. Singh vividly presented the Bolly World scenario using the narrative construction of a classic Bollywood movie script, casting the hero as India, the heroine as the foreign investment community, the villain as complacency and lack of long-term vision, and the childhood friends initially left behind by the hero as the less vibrant LDCs. In the screen drama everything looks reasonably rosy by the interval, 2015, but the hero's fortunes sour as the movie draws to its close. The next, and "worst," scenario, Atakta Bharat ("India Stumbling") was presented by Rajiv Kumar, Chief Economist of the CII. Under Atakta Bharat, things go sour much faster, in part due to a rise in adverse global conditions, including a rise in US protectionism, a European economic downturn and an increase in jihadism that requires more military spending. India's economic reforms slow, and some reforms, such as electricity market liberalization, get reversed. Growth slows to 5–6 percent by 2015 and thereafter gradually reverts to the historically low "Hindu rate of growth." Foreign direct investment declines, unemployment rises, and social and political instability increases. The picture Kumar painted of Atakta Bharat was a dark one, representing effectively what a confluence of poor policy choices and negative external conditions might produce.

The last, and "best" scenario, Pahale India ("India first"), was presented by Arun Maira, Chairman of Boston Consulting Group (India). Under Pahale India, India undertakes a proactive, integrated policy approach of inclusive development, of approaching India's policy needs as a socially, politically, economically integrated whole. PAHALE, Hindi for "first," doubles as an acronym for Poverty alleviation, Agriculture and rural development, Healthcare, Access to education, Leapfrogging infrastructure constraints, Effective governance. The policy priority under Pahale India is to treat India's growing working-age population not as a burden but as a resource, by developing a "morals of production" that creates jobs and makes young workers earners before they become consumers. Maira quoted Mahatma Gandhi's view: "people are the resource, change is for the people." By implementing Pahale India, poverty can be reduced to 7 percent of the population by 2025, and India will be in a much stronger position to weather a global economic downturn. The key differentiator between the scenarios, Maira argued, is governance. The challenge for India's leaders is to put India as a whole ahead of personal and sectoral interests. To succeed, democracy requires more than just its hardware: its parliaments and institutions. It requires software too: what people need to do themselves to make democracy work. India needs to show the world the software of democracy. Following Maira's consecration of Pahale India as the objective of the summit, Dr Montek Ahluwalia, Deputy Chairman of the Government of India's Planning Commission, reflected upon the scenarios and articulated to the attendees specifically how they should use the scenario research, namely to make and implement policies in the expectation that shorter-term policy choices will have longer-term results. Ahluwalia was able to reflect a senior Indian government policy perspective, as the Planning Commission is the government's economic policy organ.[29] Noting that the CII, as might be expected, treats Pahale India as the most likely scenario, Ahluwalia regarded Bolly World and Atakta Bharat as warnings of the consequences of policy inaction. Atakta Bharat, he argued, will not happen because governance has improved: since the early 1990s the government has become sufficiently responsive to problems that it can implement corrective policies. This has resulted from the development of increased feedback loops from civil society and political parties, all of which can appear dysfunctional and frustrating to technocrats, but which nonetheless do work successfully. Following Ahluwalia's commentary, questions from the floor sought his views on whether India's coalition politics would permit growth to accelerate from 8 percent to 10 percent per annum; and on the role of women in India's development.

The scenario session was followed immediately after lunch by the important participatory agenda-setting town-hall format session, entitled "India Town Hall: Becoming a Top-ten Competitive Economy in Ten Years." As in the Global Town Hall meeting held eleven months earlier at Davos, electronic voting equipment was placed at each seat so that instant opinion polling could be employed as part of the methodology of the session. The objective of the session, which was chaired by senior BBC foreign correspondent Nik Gowing, a longtime observer of and participant in Forum events, was to compare perceptions of India's global competitiveness held by the participants with public perceptions measured by an NDTV public opinion survey. The questions asked concerned which should be the highest priorities for the private sector and for government in advancing India's competitiveness. Before the instant polling was carried out, the Forum's Chief Economist and Director of the Global Competitiveness Programme, Augusto Lopez-Claros, framed the terms of the debate by highlighting that in the 2005–6 *Global Competitiveness Report* (*GCR*) India ranked only 50th out of 117 countries measured. India needs to improve competitiveness to improve economic growth, he argued, and growth is required to enhance opportunity, reduce poverty and build human capital. The *GCR* identified education (in particular, education of girls), infrastructure (in particular, transport and power), and the high public sector deficit as the main challenges in India's quest to improve competitiveness. In the instant polling, participants at the session identified infrastructure as the most important barrier to competitiveness that business needed to address, and highlighted the need for government to address infrastructure as well. The tables filling the room, at which seating was unassigned, were then divided up into four groups, with each group charged with discussing one of four questions, concerning how government and business respectively could act best to improve infrastructure and access to ICTs. Through a system of rapporteurs, each table's conclusions were gathered and synthesized by the chair, who summarized the conclusions for the whole assembly. For example, the general conclusion as to how best business could improve infrastructure was by deregulating through public-private partnerships, improving transparency, and sharing risks and responsibilities, all of which should reduce infrastructure bottlenecks.[30] The session was an important follow-on to the scenario presentations, in that it forced participants to engage with one another in understanding and agreeing upon objectives for the summit, and established a common language and understandings about how to debate possible means for achieving those objectives.

The rest of the panels and plenary sessions over the following days featured a star-studded succession of presentations, speakers and debates. Later on Sunday afternoon, the India Brand Equity Foundation (IBEF), a joint venture of the CII and the Indian Ministry of Commerce to promote foreign direct investment in and trade with India, presented a sparkling three-minute promotional video packed with pulsing music and fast-cutting clips of images of Indian industry, technology, infrastructure, culture and society, including figures holding dharma wheels, all supporting IBEF's marketing slogan "India: fastest growing free market democracy." Introducing Indian Finance Minister P. Chindambaram, Klaus Schwab described how India had changed over twenty-one Delhi meetings. For the first ten meetings, he said, business leaders came to complain, and government leaders came to tell business what to do. Today, according to Schwab, public-private partnerships are emerging, entrepreneurship is at the base of social progress, and the urban-rural divide is receding, with business at the core of rural development. For his part, Chindambaram gave a dynamic speech arguing that government should leave entrepreneurial activity to entrepreneurs and focus on government's other priorities. Chindambaram made a point of highlighting that Pakistan is poised to join the ranks of Asia's high-growth economies, which are driving economic growth worldwide. Later in the day still, in a session on "India and the World", Supachai Panitchpakdi, who had appeared at Davos eleven months earlier leading the WTO, spoke at Delhi as the new Director General of UNCTAD, arguing that a new geography of global trade is beginning to emerge, as one third of global trade now takes place between developing countries. This growth of "South-South" trade is largely due to the rise of the "BRICs" (Brazil-Russia-India-China), Supachai argued. It points the way to a growth path for India, because India is still underperforming its global trade potential due to incomplete integration of many domestic sectors into the global economy. According to Supachai, India in particular needs to keep reforming domestic agriculture in order to commercialize it. Indians should be thinking of exporting agricultural products, such as dairy produce, to the European Union.

The panel sessions were also striking in the range of business and economic, political and social topics that they covered and how effectively these agendas are integrated by the Forum in their focus on India. The following examples give an indication of this reach. At a panel on "Media and Entertainment: Opening the Window to the World," Michelle Guthrie, CEO of News Corporation's Hong Kong-based Star Group and a Forum Young Global Leader, argued that the Indian economy has not yet fully unlocked the value of its media and entertainment industry, which has only reached 1.5 percent of GDP, in contrast to the US industry's 5 percent. Guthrie asked why foreign investment and tax rules should be different for the cable, satellite TV and telecoms industries, and called for them to be harmonized. At the "India and the US: Emerging Global Partners" panel, US Undersecretary of Commerce David McCormick highlighted the growing importance of the US-India bilateral relationship, noting that since 2002 US exports to India had nearly doubled from $4 billion to around $7.5 billion annually. A bilateral agreement between the two governments signed on 18 July 2005 included, among other things, undertakings to cooperate on civil nuclear and energy security, high technology and space research, and increased military cooperation. The Tuesday morning session "The Gender Gap: Working Together to Improve India's Competitiveness," addressed the extent to which India's underutilization of the human capital of its women is a barrier to improving competitiveness. Using the Forum's major research report "Women's Empowerment: Measuring the Global Gender Gap" as a framework, Forum Chief Economist Augusto Lopez-Claros again used electronic voting technology to poll the participants. The polling found that, among other things, 66 percent of attendees strongly favoured setting parliamentary quotas in India for women, 26 percent favoured it and only 7 percent opposed. Delhi's Chief Minister Sheila

Dikshit commented that after achieving substantial gains for women in leadership roles in local government under Rajiv Gandhi, debate on reserving parliamentary seats for women had continued but with no action. Pakistani social entrepreneur Roshaneh Zafar highlighted the growing deficit in female births and girl babies in India due to gender-selective abortion and differential infant medical treatment. This major problem began to be featured by global media a month after the summit had ended, giving a further indication of the Forum's influence on the relationship between social issues like gender and economic development.

A full list of summit panels and plenaries is shown in Table 4.1 below.

Although the primary focus of the summit was upon India, delegates from its South Asian neighbours Sri Lanka and Pakistan were also very active participants. Senior business leaders from each country sponsored working lunches at which the economic, political and social environment in each country was discussed. Sri Lankan delegates wanted to communicate the message that, as they continued the recovery and reconstruction from the December 2004 tsunami, and despite uncertainties following the recent election of a new government led by Mahinda Rajapaksa, Sri Lanka was open for business. At the Pakistan lunch, the twin stories were Pakistan's economic reforms and emerging economic boom, as GDP growth hit 8.4 percent in 2004, and the driving role of business in warming India-Pakistan ties. Humayun Murad, CEO of Orix Leasing, one of Pakistan's largest firms, urged business leaders in both countries to bring pressure on their governments to liberalize regulations to facilitate cross-border joint ventures and to regularize bilateral trade. Ajit Gulabchand, Chairman and Managing Director of India's Hindustan Construction and the head of the Forum's Disaster Resource Network in India, said the DRN in India had been among the first to offer aid to Pakistan after the October 2005 earthquake, and it has led to the founding of a DRN in Pakistan as well. Such business altruism would end up benefiting Indian firms economically, Gulabchand argued, as Pakistan "will be a great new market." The natural mixing of public and private agendas was very much in evidence. At one of the luncheon tables, at which Indian, Pakistani and other delegates were scattered randomly, a representative of an Indian electrical goods company asked a Pakistani businessman at the table how to find a distributor for his firm's products in Pakistan. The Pakistani offered to assist him in locating the correct Pakistani chamber of commerce that could identify a suitable distributor. Business cards were exchanged,

Table 4.1 World Economic Forum 2005 India Economic Summit: topics of plenary sessions and panel discussions

27.11.2005	India and the World
27.11.2005	India and the World: Scenarios to 2025
27.11.2005	India Town Hall: Becoming a Top-ten Competitive Economy in Ten Years
27.11.2005	The Indian Economy: 8% and Beyond
28.11.2005	Energy Security: India Unplugged?
28.11.2005	Environment: Time to Clean Up
28.11.2005	Financial Services: Scaling Global Heights
28.11.2005	Foreign Direct Investment: Boom Times Ahead?
28.11.2005	From Brains to Business: Future Knowledge-based Industries
28.11.2005	Global Challenges and India
28.11.2005	Health and R&D: Harnessing India's Brain Power
28.11.2005	India and the US: Emerging Global Partners
28.11.2005	India: The New Paradigm
28.11.2005	Infrastructure: So Who Is Building the Growth Highway?
28.11.2005	Judicial Reforms: Keeping Up with an Accelerating Economy
28.11.2005	Reinventing Manufacturing
28.11.2005	Special Economic Zones: India's Best Kept Secret?
28.11.2005	Unlocking the Potential of India's Agribusiness
29.11.2005	Can Argumentative India Be Governed?
29.11.2005	Growth in an Era of Global Competition
29.11.2005	India's Talent Pyramid: Time to Rebuild?
29.11.2005	India and the Middle East: Looking Beyond
29.11.2005	Indian States: Tigers in the Making?
29.11.2005	Insights from the Co-chairs
29.11.2005	Media and Entertainment: Opening the Window to the World
29.11.2005	Pakistan: Investment and Reconstruction
29.11.2005	Sri Lanka: A Business Perspective
29.11.2005	The Gender Gap: Working Together to Improve India's Competitiveness
29.11.2005	The Indian Retail Industry: David versus Goliath?
29.11.2005	Tourism and Hospitality: Rolling Out the Red Carpet
29.11.2005	ICT in India: Time for Version 2.0?

Source: World Economic Forum.

and cross-border business ties between two former adversaries took another small step forward.

The evenings were occasions for a different mix of the social and business objectives of the summit. The first evening was launched by a drinks reception in the Taj Palace gardens hosted by the Forum's members from India. Then followed dinner in one of the hotel ballrooms with a multimedia cultural presentation sponsored by participants from Sri Lanka. Entertaining videos, song and dance performances were interspersed with short oral presentations about the revival of tourism in Sri Lanka, culminating in a brief appearance by the newly appointed Sri Lankan minister for tourism. The second, rather more ambitious evening was emceed by India's energetic and highly charismatic Minister of Commerce, Kamal Nath, who warmed up the summit participants for the evening by delivering a keynote address at the Taj Palace on "India: The New Paradigm." Painting a dynamic picture of transformation and growth in the Indian economy and society, Nath argued that India's economic reforms, once driven by crises, are now popularly backed, making it possible for shifting workforce demographics to drive manufacturing and export growth. Politically, there had been a shift in focus toward improved governance and economic development. The pattern of urbanization in India had shifted too, Nath argued, as connectivity and other technology improvements was allowing for significant growth in smaller cities and towns. Nath contended that India's growth has the potential to transform the world economy over the next two decades, pointing to studies suggesting India's GDP will pass that of Spain, Korea and Canada by 2010 and Japan by 2025. After the speech, summit participants left the hotel and queued to board coaches that would transport them to an evening of Indian cultural entertainments that Nath was hosting at the Purana Qila, an historic fort originally built in the sixteenth century by emperors Humayun and Sher Shah Sur. Transferring from the coaches to jitneys to enter the lush grounds through a massive and ancient arched stone gateway, guests shortly disembarked to stroll toward the fort down a long red-carpeted avenue flanked by towering palms and lined with flaming torches. As girls in native dress strewed rose petals along the path before the advancing summiteers, enticing aromas of meats being roasted and curries being stewed wafted lazily through the warm and fragrant evening air. White and coloured spotlights illuminated stony battlements as guests approached the fort, in front of which a stage had been set up with rows of folding chairs.

Drinks were served on the sprawling lawns adjacent to the stage, and guests mingled as they awaited the beginning of the performance. Klaus and Hilde Schwab were in relaxed and buoyant mood as they chatted with Managing Director Peter Torreele and UK financier Aly Aziz, a descendant of India's Mughal emperors. All were enthusiastic as they discussed the success of the summit. Torreele commented that he had signed up two new firms to be Industry Partners of the Forum, and Schwab had signed on international advertising giant WPP as a new Strategic Partner. Klaus Schwab recounted a humorous story about his early days at the Forum illustrating the Forum's high visibility from its inception. He told of asking his secretary to get Giscard d'Estaing on the phone for him, thinking of Olivier Giscard d'Estaing, who was working closely with the Forum at the time, only to have the call come through to his desk from Olivier's brother Valéry, who was then President of France. Schwab laughed that he was so surprised and embarrassed that he hung up on President Giscard straightaway! Soon guests were summoned to their seats, and Commerce Minister Nath took to the evening stage, morphing effortlessly into his compère role, welcoming guests "rock star" style, showering the Forum's South Asia Director Colette Mathur with praise for her role in making the summits so successful, and introducing the programme of entertainments. Against the tastefully illuminated backdrop of the old stone fort's crumbling crenellations, there then followed a lavish programme of music and dance intended to tell an historical narrative of Indian political economy and commerce. Three dance sets depicted different historical periods, commencing with a sensual, flowing *vinyasa* of yoga postures by the fit and talented dance troupe to represent ancient India, and concluding with a contemporary tableau set to pulsing Punjabi dance beats, in which the dancers manipulated giant puppets. Following the show, guests moved toward long marquees on the lawns to partake of a sumptuous banquet that featured three regional cuisines of India (Hyderabad, Lucknow and Kashmir) and continental specialities. To enjoy their meal, diners could choose between torchlit tables on the lawn or open-sided, carpeted marquees strewn with puffy cushions. As if in a fitting climax to a beautifully presented evening of India's hospitality for the Forum guests, the skies were periodically lit up by fireworks from nearby weddings taking place at the height of the astrologically favourable wedding season.

At the closing session of the summit on Tuesday the 29th, Hilde Schwab presented the Social Entrepreneur of the Year Award for India, with its accompanying membership in the Schwab Foundation and invitation to attend the Davos Annual Meeting, to a young doctor who had founded a chain of hospitals to serve the poor. The summit culminated with a concluding address to a packed hall by Indian Prime Minister Manmohan Singh. Singh recapped India's journey of reform and growth over the past two decades in the context of the socially inclusive vision of growth articulated at the "Town Hall" and "Top Ten in Ten Years" sessions of the first day, expressing concern that the media today do not show sufficient recognition of the government's commitment to rooting growth in an equitable, just society:

We have ambitions of being an economic superpower. This cannot be on a base where half our people are illiterate; where people do not have access to basic health facilities; where people do not have incomes in times of distress. In the long run, we must carry everyone along on this road to prosperity.[31]

It is safe to say that participants left the summit in Delhi, whether for locations across the city or across the world, energized by a fuller sense of the remarkable accomplishments of and major challenges facing India, with new ideas and perspectives on a range of problems affecting India and the world, and a briefcase full of new or renewed business and social contacts.

5   Discourse, research and action
Technology and the Initiatives

Introduction

This chapter reflects in greater depth upon the knowledge, information and ideas that the World Economic Forum creates and exchanges. It begins by looking at how the Forum uses words and ideas to contribute to the development of major public discourses, and in doing so how the Forum has helped to frame the choices faced in the contemporary global political, economic and social environment. It then considers the particular role of information technology in the Forum's project of discursive construction. The heart of the chapter focuses on the Forum's research and action output: its publications and its more recent forays into public-private partnerships for "improving the state of the world:" the Initiatives.

The discourse of the Forum: defining terms, constructing realities

The World Economic Forum has shown as well as any organization that words and ideas matter. Words and ideas make discourse, which frames how people understand their environment and possibilities for change. The Forum's core functions are about generating, exchanging and debating knowledge and ideas. More latterly, as is discussed later in this chapter, it has been about experimenting with ways to operationalize these ideas. But the process of generating and debating ideas is a process of discursive construction in which participants propose, argue over, and come to prefer some words, some understandings, some ideas over others. As Forum members and invited participants often hold considerable power in the global political economy, the Forum's processes of discursive construction have to be viewed as having a shaping influence on the linguistic and ideational terrain upon which social forces and political and economic actors must operate. The terms and understandings that actors share, and the possibilities for action that flow therefrom (and other possibilities that become by definition excluded) are going to be defined in part by the Forum's discursive project. Whilst space does not permit a full mapping of the Forum's impact upon this global linguistic and ideational terrain, discussion of a few of the key terms upon which the Forum has had an impact should suffice to illustrate this point.

Perhaps the most important example of the Forum's discursive impact is the idea of globalization itself. It was around competing, alternate understandings of globalization and its possibilities that the competing "Shar-pei" and "Wolf in Sheep's Clothing" narratives of the Forum's evolution emerged. Although the World Economic Forum was founded well before globalization was being discussed as such, the Forum was initially a product of, and thereafter a driver of, the particular set of economic, social and political phenomena now understood as globalization. From its inception the Forum represented a convergence between European and North American models of relations between business and government.[1] If the model of business-government relations in Western Europe that succeeded in rebuilding the postwar West European economies was built around tripartite cooperation at the nation-state level between government, management and labor, orchestrated by national and local governments (often through government ownership of the commanding heights of the industrial economy), the US model was built around greater distance between management on the one hand and government and labor on the other. Whereas the European model may have produced greater consent of the governed within civil society in each nation-state, the US model gave the managements of US-based firms greater flexibility to take advantage of improvements to the global production chain from innovation in transport and communications by making acquisitions, joint ventures, trade and investments.[2] At the Forum's inception, Klaus Schwab was keen to bring these US management techniques and approaches to Europe. The fledgling European Management Forum can be understood as an attempt by managements of European firms in the first instance to take a more leading role independent of the traditional nation-state-level European tripartite government-management-labor relationship in shaping future relations between firms and between firms and governments. Importantly, it also enabled European managers to undertake this project at a pan-European and subsequently global level.

Once in operation the Forum began to advance the interests of its member firms by carrying out its public and private agendas of identifying and debating the world's major economic and social problems, creating and sponsoring new venues for public-private cooperation, and hosting gatherings at which transnational business deals could be done. In part resulting from their participation in Forum events and activities, Forum member firms increasingly came to favour public policies that would enable them not only to profit more from integration of the global production chain and a global marketplace, such as advancing macroeconomic and monetary policy cooperation, promoting harmonization of commercial regulations, and removing regulatory impediments to free flows of trade and investment. But they also embraced policies that would shape the nature of the global marketplace in various ways that both benefited the firms and created public, social benefits as well. By expanding the range of its interlocutors and participants to include first government officials and then representatives of major other multilateral, nongovernmental and civil society organizations, and extending the scope of its activities to include promoting regional and interregional economic, business and political cooperation and information exchange, the Forum was in effect directly promoting a version of globalization centring around market opening and convergence and that was favourable to its member firms. Although promotion of official instances and venues of public-private cooperation and providing venues for business deals is an important part of promoting globalization, perhaps the most significant structural sense in which the Forum has done so is through the creation of networks for information exchange and mutual education of members and participants. The use of cutting-edge information technology has played a central role in the Forum's promotion of information exchange.

Beyond pursuing a globalization agenda that has promoted particular convergence and market liberalization objectives, however, the Forum has promoted the development of the discourse of globalization that by the late 1990s came to attract attention not only among scholars but among the media, governments and civil society generally. For the Forum this result of its activities has been a double-edged sword. A discourse can be seen in a number of ways: as a set of public utterances or texts; a series of interactions, debates, discussions and decisions in the public space. Discourses contain underlying meanings and relations of power and often serve as tableaux in which the interests of dominant powers are fulfilled and consecrated publicly. However, by their nature public discourses also contain possibilities for transformation of interests and outcomes through contest with alternate and opposing views, interests and power groupings.[3] By growing in influence and importance through the promotion of information exchange, the Forum drew attention to the private interests of its members in a public way, even whilst operating under the aegis of providing a public service to businesses, governments and other actors (whether members of the Forum or not).

After the Cold War ended (an end which the Forum openly claims a role in achieving), the global marketplace was formally reunified in a political sense. This transformation ushered in the period generally bounded at its ends by 9 November 1989, the date of the fall of the Berlin Wall ("11/9"), and the al-Qa'eda attacks of 11 September 2001 ("9/11") and sometimes now referred to as the "11/9 to 9/11" period. The 11/9 to 9/11 period was characterized by vigorous growth of structures of neoliberal capitalism of the Thatcher-Reagan variety and their spread across the former socialist economies "in transition." As the 1990s progressed, "globalization" became the byword, the catchphrase for this amorphous set of economic, social and political phenomena. What was important was that people across the world were creating it, constructing it, by talking about it in particular ways in the media, in houses of parliament, in corporate boardrooms and strategy seminars at marketing firms, and in meetings of many civil society organizations who officially were committed to resisting the very phenomena they in fact were participating in reifying. This globalization discourse came to dominate the attention of scholars in relevant fields and of policymakers in governments, multilateral organizations and CSOs. The themes of the Davos Annual Meetings in the 1990s illustrates how extensively the Forum embraced the globalization discourse at its point of highest visibility and how the tone already began to shift from 2000.[4]

World Economic Forum Davos Annual Meeting themes from 1991– 2001 have been as follows:

1991 The new direction for global leadership
1992 Global cooperation and megacompetition
1993 Rallying all the forces for global recovery
1994 Redefining the basic assumptions of the world economy
1995 Challenges beyond growth
1996 Sustaining globalization
1997 Building the Network Society
1998 Priorities for the twenty-first century
1999 Managing the impact of globalization
2000 New beginnings: making a difference
2001 Sustaining growth and bridging the divides: a framework for our global future.

The themes of this 11/9/89–9/11/01 period reflected objectives shared by many Forum member firms of meeting and overcoming obstacles to the advancement of a barrier-free global marketplace supported by compliant governments and civil society. By the end of the 1990s and even more so after 9/11, this construction of globalization came to be contested increasingly by growing segments of global civil society (see Chapter 6).

Ironically, whilst no doubt some members of the Forum choose to belong primarily for the private networking opportunities that membership permits, many member firms choose to participate because they value the Forum's public-private partnership objectives and see the Forum as the most attractive venue for engaging in global corporate citizenship. For their part, the senior managers of the Forum had long been on record as endorsing a version of corporate citizenship that embraced social responsibility, as attested to from the beginning by Klaus Schwab's multi-stakeholder model and articulated at the beginning of the 1990s by the Forum motto "entrepreneurship in the global public interest." Yet from the beginning of the 2000s the Forum had to focus its attention on reconstructing the idea of globalization discursively in such a way as to re-legitimate it for the many for whom it had lost credibility. In the themes of the Davos panels there was a discernible shift in direction within just a few years. In 1998 panels focused on global monetary policy on investments and capital flows (in the wake of the 1997 Asian financial crisis); regulating the internet; Islamic fundamentalism; resistance to the European single currency; and the debate between the neoliberal and European statist models of political economy. By contrast, the 2001 Davos agenda featured panels on themes such as:

- How can globalization deliver the goods – the view from the South
- The corporation and the public – open for inspection
- Addressing the backlash against globalization
- Seizing the global digital opportunity
- Business and NGOs: from diatribe to dialogue
- Whatever happened to sustainable development?
- Leapfrogging with technology to alleviate poverty.[5]

One of the principal conclusions reached at the 2001 Davos Panel on the corporation and the public encapsulated the apparent shift of focus among Forum members succinctly: "In the face of increasing public concern and fear about corporate power and influence in all aspects of life, companies must take into account the expectations of the public."[6]

Whilst globalization is probably the most important and most contested discursive term to be constructed by the Forum, others are also significant. The idea of public-private partnership, which is at the core of the Forum's methodologies for solving problems and improving global governance, and the idea of global governance itself, to which it is closely linked, have been constructed in important ways by the Forum's processes and activities. Public-private partnership was originally identified more closely with the post-World War II European social consensus on the shared roles and responsibilities of government, business and labour that Klaus Schwab set out to shake up with the European Management Forum in the interest of making European business more competitive globally in the 1970s. It was seen as a more socially and politically palatable alternative to the more adversarial notion of social relations between economic classes that had previously been embraced both by business and capital and by labor unions and Marxist intellectuals.

Far from the postwar West German model of industrial co-determination, Klaus Schwab's multi-stakeholder approach had the same objective, but it imagined a much more flexible architecture of public-private cooperation that would allow for variable geometries of actor participation and processes undertaken. The key to the Forum's idea of public-private partnerships was that they would be based upon the best possible management techniques. Through the development of the Initiatives, the Forum has constructed the idea of public-private partnerships to be flexible, task-oriented and results-driven. Public-private partnerships organized by the Forum take very different forms according to the objective pursued, and they are comprised of a wide range of different public and private actors, including governments, global and local or regional firms, civil society organizations and multilateral institutions. The Forum also has played a pivotal and as yet largely unheralded role in constructing a notion of global governance that, as it is emerging, is coming to be accepted and perceived to have a measure of legitimacy by civil society, as opposed to being seen as strictly as a version of global corporatism that normalizes the dominance of global capital. This measure of legitimacy appears to derive in large part from the flexible architecture and variable geometries of public-private partnerships and the project-oriented nature of the cooperation that the Forum seeks to catalyze. Whether creating a technology-intensive model for national education system reforms, facilitating compromise in multilateral agricultural trade negotiations, or constructing a network of firms, governments and civil society organizations to respond to natural disasters, Forum public-private partnerships contributing to global governance are not centrally managed from above, and thus hope to avoid the tag of an incipient world federalism that enshrines one set of interests over those of others.

A third discursive construction upon which the Forum has made a major impact is social and political notions of belonging. Association with, or belonging to, the World Economic Forum is not like belonging to other entities, whether they be private clubs, multilateral organizations, firms, civil society organizations or nation-states. As the Forum has developed, this difference has become steadily greater, and it has significant implications for how we understand the idea of belonging in contemporary global society. After beginning with an initial model of inviting businesspeople to come to Davos, for a fee, the Forum reconstituted itself as a membership organization in 1976. Members received particular privileges, in terms of places at meetings, and later research output, in return for paying an annual fee. But even as membership became the basis on which the Forum would operate, and would finance its undertakings, a clear dichotomy between membership and non-membership could never emerge. Differentiation of standing in terms of participation at Davos and subsequently at other meetings had already been introduced from 1973, when political leaders began to be invited to participate as guests. This differentiation was an inescapable consequence of the multi-stakeholder approach, and it continued to develop, as the Forum invited more different types of stakeholders to participate in Forum activities in the 1980s: academics, media, artists, civil society organizations, etc. In the 1990s, the Forum began to differentiate membership itself, offering different levels of participation in the planning and management of Forum events and research, and even of the Forum itself, in the form of what it dubbed partnerships. By the 2000s, the Forum began to describe, and to constitute, the different types of stakeholders routinely invited to attend the Forum as communities, which were given recognized identities, opportunities to meet, generate ideas and make policy recommendations to the Forum, at Davos and at other times. Beyond the communities, the Forum gave distinct identities to additional classes of participants, by creating bodies such as the Forum for Young Global Leaders and the Schwab Foundation for Social Entrepreneurship.

This vastly differentiated, and continuously changing, topography of participation in the events and activities of the Forum is utterly different from, and poses a challenge to, more traditional, dichotomous notions of belonging to organizations, such as the United Nations, where each member state has one vote in the General Assembly, or the World Bank and International Monetary Fund, in which membership, and voting rights, is differentiated by share ownership. The very words used to invoke this differentiated topography of belonging and participating – members, partners, communities, Young Global Leaders,

Social Entrepreneurs – strive for the legitimacy that only the being-present of the participants at the Forum can confer. The longer-term implications of this emerging postmodern discourse of belonging for global society and its institutions are not yet clear.

Information technology and contesting the discourse

The World Economic Forum has always been skilled in two areas: adopting information technology and using it to tell the Forum's story to the public. By foregrounding the globalization discourse publicly in the way that it did in the 1980s and 1990s, the World Economic Forum contributed substantially to a process that has already changed the discourse of globalization in a more socially inclusive direction and may end up shifting the distribution of power in the global political economy itself. This process has led to the inclusion of a wider range of participants from civil society than the original groups of leading media figures, artists and academics invited to participate in Forum events and activities, and the contesting of the Forum members' visions of the global economy by alternate visions containing different social and economic priorities. By the late 1990s, thanks in large part to the rise of the internet, the many diverse and widely dispersed groups opposing the type of globalization that they perceived to be advocated by the Forum (many of which were very local and which had been around for many years) began to find and network with each other. They entered into the debates over globalization, which they discovered to be a favourable and relevant public space to articulate their political views and challenge existing politico-economic power structures, and they realized that events of organizations such as the Forum (and the World Trade Organization) were ideal physical loci for protest and the posing of counterarguments (see Chapter 6).[7]

The most significant, and interlocking, changes affecting the Forum resulting from its process of engagement with critics have been increased transparency, broadening of participation and a shift in the discourse, each of which has contributed to a change in the content of the Forum's public information output. Following the success of the cross-national network of opponents of the neoliberal Multilateral Agreement on Investment (see Chapter 6) in blocking its passage in 1998, nation-state governments and multilateral institutions alike began to engage more extensively with a wider range of civil society organizations and to increase transparency in global economic policy-making.[8] The Forum, which had marketed its public information output to the general public ever more aggressively in the 1990s, found that it needed to acknowledge, at least implicitly, that transparency requires a degree of surrender of control over information flows and who generates them. Greater transparency for and broader participation in a non-legislative multilateral body like the Forum can be understood as a way of democratization of a process of global economic policymaking without voting or legislating. Senior executives of the Forum would argue that this has always been at the core of their objectives. O'Brien *et al.* describe this process as "complex multilateralism," a hybridization of state-centric and civil society-driven multilateral cooperation in which institutional change has so far exceeded real policy reform.[9]

At the beginning of the 2001 Davos Annual Meeting, Charles McLean, then the World Economic Forum's Director of Communications, stated in a television interview with BBC reporter Nik Gowing that the Forum had taken the agenda of the protesters on board and urged protesters to participate in the debates inside the Centre des Congrès, arguing that decisions get taken inside, not in the streets.[10] The public proceedings of the Davos meeting took a quantum leap forward in terms of transparency, again driven by information and communications technology. The Forum's public access website for the 2001 Davos Annual Meeting was upgraded substantially over that for 2000 to include live and recorded webcasts of Davos panel discussions, as well as bulletin boards for the general public to make and read comments on each panel theme. Like the citizen networks, the Forum began to use the internet to encourage a two-way dialogue with the public, using approaches such as creating a Forum blog. Thus there was if anything a competitive convergence between the Forum and their opponents in the use of internet technology to communicate to the general public their objectives and the content of their public-facing activities. The greater transparency that the Forum has embraced has also illuminated more clearly the boundary between the Forum's public and private information output, and may or may not have shifted that boundary in the direction whereby more of the private understandings, negotiations and deals done at Davos are also (even if not immediately) revealed to the public.

Research and action: the Global Competitiveness Programme

More than just a conference planner

For an organization that from the start was all about generating and exchanging knowledge and information, the production and dissemination of research was a natural and inevitable evolution for the Forum. From the early years Klaus Schwab was concerned that the Forum develop the capacity to contribute more to the process of solving global problems than just the ideas generated at its summits and other meetings. He was also concerned that the Forum begin to utilize the collective resources of its staff and membership to provide more to members than just efficient planning of conferences. Hence what began with the decision to produce an annual research report on the competitiveness of nation-states has grown steadily into a major component of the Forum's activities. Research into competitiveness has grown into the Global Competitiveness Programme, of which the flagship publication is the annual *Global Competitiveness Report* (*GCR*), but which also comprises the publication of several annual regional and sectoral competitiveness reports and other publications. Another venture was an annual magazine to feature thought pieces about global issues of concern by political, business and civil society leaders and by academics, tying in with each year's Davos meeting. The magazine, introduced titled as *World Link* in 1988, is published in London by the Forum in collaboration with Euromoney plc and is known today as *Global Agenda*. Circulated to attendees at Davos and available to others by subscription, *Global Agenda* probably has the biggest and most illustrious list of contributors of any publication in the world. It is filled with ideas and arguments on topics in geopolitics and security, economics and finance, business and management, science and technology, and culture and values. The Forum's research has subsequently expanded into numerous ongoing fixed-term research projects, which the Forum has dubbed Initiatives, and which have been undertaken in collaboration with other institutions ranging from multilateral economic institutions such as the World Bank to think tanks and academic institutions to individual country governments (see below).

The Forum's foray into research began in 1979, when Klaus Schwab proposed to the Executive Board that the Forum utilize the economic expertise of its staff to produce a research report for members of the Forum that evaluated the competitiveness of sixteen European nations. The first edition, titled the *Report on the Competitiveness of European Industry 1979*, was circulated to members attending the Davos meeting in January 1980 as a supporting document for the meeting's theme, "An Agenda for European Business Leaders: International Cooperation, Productivity, and Social Commitment." Schwab's initial conception of the business model for the report was that it would be one of the perquisites of membership, thereby expanding members' benefits beyond the opportunity to attend Forum conferences.[11] He envisaged making the report available for purchase by non-members for a high market price, initially over $1000, but the subsequently the Forum chose to publish the Report in collaboration with commercial publishers and market it to the general public. The 2005–6 *Global Competitiveness Report* was available for purchase commercially for $110, with past editions marked down accordingly (2004–5 for $85, etc.).[12]

What was perhaps the most startling about the Forum's competitiveness research was that it ranked countries in league tables of how competitive they were relative to others in the survey. But the Forum's approach to competitiveness of nation-states did not adopt a narrowly neoliberal definition of the most barrier-free business climate, instead embracing a more comprehensive, social definition in keeping with the Forum's multi-stakeholder approach to governance. In Jeffrey Sachs and Andrew M. Warner's lead essay in the 1996 edition of the *GCR*, entitled "Why Competitiveness Counts," they define competitiveness as "the ability of a nation's economy to make rapid and sustained gains in living standards."[13] National competitiveness was articulated in the *GCR* more as a proxy for a broader, socioeconomic understanding of economic development. Schwab's original conception was that the report assess competitiveness using both traditional quantitative measures, such as productivity and costs of production, and more qualitative, intersubjective measures such as quality of human resources and sociopolitical consensus.[14] In Professor Schwab's view, the business climate of a country was as important to judging its ability to be competitive in a global marketplace as quantitative measures of economic achievement. A business climate is fundamentally about perceptions held by those who make decisions about where and how to invest, produce, sell and govern. Thus whereas the quantitative measures could be taken through the gathering and processing of statistical data, taking qualitative measures required interviews with CEOs, economists and other relevant actors in national economies. The qualitative research evolved into an annual Executive Opinion Survey, which the Forum conducts each winter and spring by polling executives extensively on the business environment in the countries in which they operate, and on the principal obstacles to economic growth that they encountered.[15] From early on the Forum staff developed less traditional quantitative metrics to assess competitiveness, such as language proficiency of a population and effectiveness of telephone systems.[16] This presaged what would become a major focus for the Forum's assessment criteria in the areas of good governance and technological readiness.

The report evolved rapidly from its first year, when it was researched and written largely by Schwab himself. By the second year, 240 criteria for assessing competitiveness were included, and it was renamed the *Report on Industrial Competitiveness*. The number of countries assessed grew from 16 in 1979 to 104 countries by the publication of the 2004–5 edition, as the country focus expanded from Europe to the globe. As the staff demands for producing the report grew, the Forum partnered with the International Institute for Management Development (IMD), a Lausanne-based business school, for three years to produce the report from 1990, when it was retitled the *World Competitiveness Report*. The Forum brought production of the report back in house following concerns about methodology. In 1996 leading global economist Jeffrey Sachs agreed to chair an advisory board to monitor the methodological soundness of the report, which in that year was given its current name, the *Global Competitiveness Report*.[17] As the *GCR* gained acceptance and influence, the Forum began to replicate its format and methodology to produce competitiveness reports for regions and sectors. By the early 2000s, the Forum was publishing regional competitiveness reports on the Central and Eastern European economies in transition, Latin America, Africa, and the Arab states. In 2002, in keeping with their focus on the importance of technology for growth, the Forum initiated the *Global Information Technology Report*, an annual survey of the competitiveness of nations in the ICT sector.

How are the Forum's competitiveness reports used? Who reads them? Are they making an impact upon the discourse of economic development, and if so how? The methodology of creating league tables of competitiveness by country is intended to generate global standards of best practice and aspirations for performance improvement by policymakers across all the stakeholders in a given economy. Describing the Forum's hopes for the Executive Opinion Survey of business perceptions, *GCR* co-editor Xavier Sala-i-Martin argues that it "may help precipitate an internal debate within the country between government officials, business leaders, organizations of civil society and the academic community on key problem areas and how best to address them."[18] Evidence suggests that, at least in some quarters, the *GCR* is being read and taken seriously at the highest levels of business and government. At the Forum's 2005 India Economic Summit, the motivational effect of the *GCR's* league table ranking upon Indian business and political leaders was evident throughout the discourse. In the 2004–5 *GCR*, India's overall competitiveness ranking was 55th out of 104 countries, having risen one place from the previous year.[19] At the

Delhi summit business and government leaders alike discussed what would be required for India to achieve what was clearly an already mooted objective: to move India into the top ten within ten years.

The league table approach clearly plays a significant role in the motivational strategy of the Global Competitiveness Programme. The very notion of using a league table, as opposed, for example, to ratings on a numerical scale, is in a sense a competitive metaphor drawn from sport. It creates a competition to be competitive, as it were: someone must be first, someone must be last. If the headline number in a table is a country's ranking (1st, 2nd, 54th, 89th, etc.), it tends to relegate to rather more secondary importance the absolute level of whatever quantity is being measured. For example, if worker productivity were being measured across ten countries, with the first-ranked country achieving 100, it could easily be that the second-ranked country achieved 99.5 and the third-ranked country 99.2, but the fourth-ranked country achieved only 78 and the remaining six countries scored above 55. Hence the distinction between first and third in the league table would be statistically almost insignificant, whereas the distinction between third and fifth, or even third and fourth, would be enormous. All the participants in the discussion in New Delhi openly acknowledged that, irrespective of India's meeting its instrumental targets to attain top ten performance, whether it could achieve a top ten ranking was entirely contingent upon the relative competitiveness performances of other current and future major players in the league. Harvard Business School Professor Michael Porter, Co-Director of the *GCR* and who views competitiveness as a proxy for productivity, does take pains to disavow the winners/losers construction of competitiveness: "The world economy is not a zero-sum game. Many nations can improve their prosperity if they improve productivity."[20] Nonetheless the intended, and unintended, consequences of using league tables need to be investigated further.

So the Forum's methodology in the competitiveness reports plays a key role in generating and shaping the discourse of economic and social development and growth that the Forum wants to advance. Each of the competitiveness reports may be organized slightly differently, but the core components of the methodology are replicated. A blend of quantitative indicators and perceptual indicators based upon surveys of business leaders is assessed and measured to generate league tables that rank countries in terms of competitiveness. The competitiveness findings are explained discursively in text that is accessible, compact but not superficial, and intended for the general public. Scholarly articles reflecting upon the findings and different perspectives on the implications are a major component. Detailed quantitative data on the competitiveness of each country are also included, with accompanying textual explanation. What follows below is a selective analysis of discursive constructions in the *GCR* and the *Global Information Technology Report* that is intended to illuminate how the Forum uses the research to influence the discourse and set global agendas for development and growth.

The Global Competitiveness Report

The *GCR* has become known as the Forum's signature research product. Its current format includes three major sections. The first section contains the report's distinctive league tables that rank countries ordinally across a series of competitiveness metrics and from which the Report's first of two major league tables of overall competitiveness rankings, the Growth Competitiveness Index, is derived. This index is composed of an extensive aggregation of quantitative measures, with resulting ordinal rankings, of three broad components: macroeconomic environment, quality of public institutions, and technology. Within each component are major subcomponents: for example, the macroeconomic environment is comprised of macroeconomic stability, government waste, and country credit rating. The component indicators are not fixed in stone, as the Forum seeks ways to make its research more useful. The Forum made a significant change in the macroeconomic environment index in the 2003–4 *GCR* by replacing the variable "government expenditure as a percentage of GDP" with a composite measure of government waste, produced by tracking distortive government subsidies, diversion of public funds, and public trust in politicians' financial honesty. The revision was a clear shift away from neoliberalism: it was done expressly to acknowledge that government expenditure can be productive and make positive contributions to competitiveness, and to focus criticism upon cronyism and corruption.[21] The adjustment was significant enough in the generation of the overall Growth Competitiveness Index to cause Finland to edge the United States out of the number one position, both for 2003–4 and in the revised numbers for 2002–3.

The GCR's second major competitiveness ranking, the Business Competitiveness Index, is derived primarily from the subjective, perceptual element of the research, the Executive Opinion Survey, although where possible, quantitative measures of patent rates and penetration of the internet and mobile telephony are included. The Executive Opinion Survey, through which the Forum, working with regional and national partner organizations, maps perceptions of each country's business environment, in 2003–4 tabulated over 8100 responses to the largest survey conducted up to that point, with over 200 questions. A typical survey question asked: "In your country, diversion of public funds to companies, individuals, or groups due to corruption: Is Common . . . Never Occurs," requesting respondents to mark their response on a scale of 1 to 7 between the two poles.[22] Accompanying all of the league tables showing the headline indices and their components and subcomponents is explanatory and interpretive text that, among other things, comments on the movement of countries up and down the tables from past years to the present, which gives the reader some temporal context in which to interpret the data.

In the second section of the *GCR*, latterly dubbed "Selected Issues of Competitiveness," are scholarly essays that discuss topics ranging from how major issues of the day, such as governance or corporate social responsibility, affect competitiveness to reasons for the outperformance of a particular country or region. The adjacent table gives a sense of the range of topics covered in the two most recent issues. Further analysis of the discursive content of the scholarship appears below. The third section of the report contains detailed country-by-country quantitative data on competitiveness. The detailed country profile pages indicate, for each country, its ranking according to the major competitiveness indices, the Growth Competitiveness Index and the Business Competitiveness Index, and the major subcomponents of each. A bar graph charts the most problematic factors for doing business, as identified by the Executive Opinion Survey. For example, in the 2004–5 *GCR*, the largest percentages of respondents in Peru said the most problematic factors were policy instability and access to financing, whereas in the United States the greatest percentages identified tax regulations and inefficient bureaucracy. For each country there also appears a "national competitiveness balance sheet," which divides the most significant components and subcomponents of the Growth Competitiveness Index, Business Competitiveness and other important indicators for each country into two columns: notable competitive advantages, where the country has performed well, and notable competitive disadvantages, where the country has performed poorly. The country's rank for each is displayed, enabling the reader to take in at a glance how a country's competitive strengths and weaknesses according to the Forum's methodology and make judgements accordingly. Box 5.1 shows authors and titles of scholarly articles appearing in the 2004–5 *GCR*.

Throughout the text of the Global Competitiveness Reports, one can find articulations of competitiveness that are neoliberal and economistic, as well as framings that are more broadly socially inclusive and reflective of the Forum's multi-stakeholder approach. In the mid-1990s, when the *GCR* reached its current form amidst the dominance of post-Cold War neoliberal global business culture, there were numerous neoliberal discursive articulations of competitiveness in the report. In the 1996 report Sachs and Warner, for example, articulate eight structural characteristics by which to measure competitiveness: (1) openness of the economy to trade and finance; (2) the role of the government budget and regulation; (3) development of financial markets; (4) quality of infrastructure; (5) quality of technology; (6) quality of business management; (7) labour market flexibility; and (8) quality of judicial and political institutions.[23] In another chapter in the 1996 edition, Sachs and Warner blame the structure of the social welfare state for slow economic growth in Europe. They single out state pension systems for special opprobrium, implying a neoliberal preference for forcing individuals to provide for their own retirement needs through private markets: "a generous state pension reduces the need for younger generations to save for their own retirement."[24] In doing so they also criticize the inflexibility of European labour markets. In the executive summary chapter for the same edition, Frederick Hu and Jeffrey Sachs laud small, highly competitive "entrepot" economies such as Hong Kong, Luxembourg, Singapore and Switzerland. They praise New Zealand for achieving a high ranking in the league table of competitiveness by implementing over ten years a set of structural and policy reforms focused upon opening the economy, cutting back government spending, privatization of state enterprises and innovation in government fiscal policies, pensions and central banking.[25]

Yet in the same edition of the *Global Competitiveness Report* the discourse of competitiveness being generated also reflects sensitivity to the social and cultural consequences of economic growth. In "Beyond the Statistics," then Managing Director Claude Smajda observes that economic growth and advances in technology have had "a destructive impact on the overall employment picture," as the growth of robotics has eliminated hundreds of thousands of low-skilled jobs and has endangered services jobs as well. Rejecting the oft-articulated "less government is best" 1990s neoliberal business mantra, Smajda argues that in order to be solved the problem must be addressed by government and business together: "the sharing of responsibilities between the state and corporations has become the key to creating the most propitious environment for competitiveness. . . . The dialogue between business and government has to take on a new content and a new dimension."[26] For Smajda, business demands for deregulation should

Box 5.1: Authors and titles of scholarly articles appearing in the Global Competitiveness Report 2004–5.

Part 1: The Competitiveness Indexes

1.1 Policies and Institutions Underpinning Economic Growth: Results from the Competitiveness Indexes
BY AUGUSTO LOPEZ-CLAROS, JENNIFER BLANKE, MARGARETA DRZENIEK, IRENE MIA AND SAADIA ZAHID

1.2 Buliding the Microeconomic Foundations of Prosperity: Findings from the Business Competitiveness Index
BY MICHAEL E. PORTER

Part 2: Selected Issues of Competitiveness

2.1 Myths and Realities of Governance and Corruption
BY DANIEL KAUFMANN

2.2 Rethinking Exchange Rate Competitiveness
B KENNETH ROGOFF

2.3 Securing Land Property Rights in Africa: Improving the Investment Climate
BY CAMILLA TOULMIN

2.4 The Environment as a Source of Competitive Advantage
BY ALLEN L. HAMMOND

2.5 Can Europe Compete? The International and Technological Competitiveness of Europe
BY BEATRICE WEDER DI MAURO

2.6 Russia: Competitiveness, Growth, and the Next Stage of Development
BY AUGUSTO LOPEZ-CLAROS

Part 3: Special Topics

3.1 Should There Be a Development Consensus?
BY JOHN WILLIAMSON

3.2 Aging in Low-Income Countries: Looking to 2025
BY NICHOLAS EBERSTADT

3.3 Emerging Market Crises and Crisis Resolution: A Decade of Experience
BY NOURIEL ROUBINI AND BRAD SETSER

3.4 Full Employment for Europe
BY RICHARD LAYARD

3.5 Globalization as an Agent of Prosperity
BY JAGDISH BHAGWATI

Source: World Economic Forum, Global Competitiveness Report 2004-05.

not imply a return to nineteenth-century laissez-faire economics: "for competition to work – and for competitiveness to be rewarded – governments have to play their role at the national as well as at the international levels."

The Forum has also used the *GCR* to foreground its focus upon the importance of governance. Daniel Kaufmann of the World Bank Institute, writing in three successive issues of the *GCR* beginning in 2002–3, focused on the relationship between good governance and economic growth and stability. In his article "Governance Redux: The Empirical Challenge" in the *GCR 2003–4*, Kaufmann writes:

Thanks to a seachange [*sic*] at agencies such as the World Bank, as well as to the embracing of the challenge of governance by institutions such as the World Economic Forum, it is now possible to discuss openly the reality of governance worldwide, and apply such knowledge in concrete ways in countries intent on improving.[27]

According to Kaufmann, governance is at a "crossroads," lagging behind progress that has been made in macroeconomic policy reforms in developing countries, which is significant because foreign direct investment flows are more closely correlated to indicators of good governance than they are to indicators of sound macroeconomic policy. Kaufmann defined governance as "the set traditions and formal and informal institutions that determine how authority is exercised in a particular country for the common good," which can be broken down into

> (1) the process of selecting, monitoring, and replacing governments; (2) the capacity to formulate and implement sound policies and deliver public services; and (3) the respect of citizens and the state for the institutions that govern economic and social interactions among them.[28]

To develop empirical measures of governance for purposes of comparison and ranking, Kaufmann broke these three categories into six testable metrics (voice and external accountability; political stability and lack of violence, crime and terrorism; government effectiveness; lack of regulatory burden; rule of law; and control of corruption), from which he was able to generate absolute scores and ordinal league tables.[29] Analysis of the data documented the important conclusion that good governance promoted economic growth and development, but that wealth did not of itself promote good governance.[30] Kaufmann used these and other findings to argue for the increased use of empirical research on governance to underpin the Forum's case for promoting good governance as a key instrument for stimulating economic development and growth.

As the *Global Competitiveness Report*, and the Forum's research capacities, have evolved, the Forum staff have been able to increase the *GCR*'s value added by making the content of the analytical articles responsive to major world events affecting the global economy, often on very short notice. The analysis in the *GCR* places impact of events such as 9/11/01 and the December 2004 South Asian tsunami in the context of the Forum's overall multi-stakeholder approach to global problem solving. By interpreting such events for its readers within its own discursive framework, the Forum is able to contribute to the formation of perceptions of problems and possible policy responses by senior policymakers in business and government. The *Global Competitiveness Report 2001–2* was already in the editorial stage of publication when the attacks of 11 September 2001 occurred, but the

Forum rapidly pulled the document from editorial for major reworking. In the revised report, which was published in early 2002, the analytical discussion focused intensively on the impact of the attacks on the global economy. Within three weeks of the plane crashes, the Forum conducted what it called a "flash survey" of ninety senior executives of member companies of the Forum, to get an initial sense of the impact of 9/11 upon business and consumer confidence. The broad general findings of the flash survey showed that the attacks "had a slightly but not overwhelmingly negative effect on consumer confidence," suggesting greater resilience in the global economy than might have been expected. The survey also found business perceptions of economic conditions following 9/11 to be similar across the globe, providing further evidence for understanding international business as operating in a fully globalized economic space.[31] In his preface to the 2001–2 *GCR*, Klaus Schwab argued that confidence-building measures were needed to stimulate both consumer and corporate demand. Schwab's concern was that the attacks could lead to a retreat from government and business commitments to global economic flows, which could affect all participants adversely. His prescriptions centred on the importance of preserving, reinforcing and strengthening the structures of global production chains and trade flows, arguing that a coordinated international governmental economic response to 9/11 "must involve bolstering the framework of globalization and recommitting governments around the world to making the world economy work for all nations, including the poorest."[32] Schwab made six specific policy recommendations by which the public sector could achieve these objectives:

1 Governments: continue diplomacy to avoid a major global military conflict.
2 Governments: increase confidence in cross-border flows by strengthening trade, transport and travel security.
3 OPEC: continue to make supply decisions so as to avoid disruption in oil supplies.
4 Central banks: continue to ensure ample monetary liquidity to avoid deflation.
5 Governments: launch a new multilateral trade liberalization round at the November 2002 WTO ministerial to increase poor countries' access to industrial country markets and improve access to essential medicines.
6 US government: reform and increase its aid to developing countries to improve health and reduce social unrest and violence in poor countries.[33]

Schwab's focus here is on the socioeconomic conditions that are causes of violence and terrorism, the ability of global economic growth and development to ameliorate those conditions, and the ability of governments and public institutions to enable and facilitate equitable and sustainable growth.

The Global Information Technology Report

The *Global Information Technology Report* (*GITR*) takes a slightly different approach from that of the global and regional competitiveness reports, exploring in greater depth the relationship between information and communication technologies and economic growth and development, across a global range of countries. The *GITR* had its roots in the G-8's Digital Opportunity Task Force, which was established at the Okinawa/Kyushu summit in July 2000.[34] The first report was released in 2001–2, immediately following the crash of the 1990s technology boom, and was the product of collaborative research between the Forum, the European business school INSEAD, and the World Bank-sponsored infoDev group, itself a partnership of different organizations that is dedicated to using ICTs to fight poverty and promote economic growth in developing countries.[35] Like its elder sibling the *Global Competitiveness Report*, the *GITR* is intended to promote best practices in government and business, in this case in the use and application of ICTs, through benchmarking, the creation of league tables. Klaus Schwab articulated the *GITR's* objectives succinctly in the preface to the 2003–4 edition:

> Recognizing the importance of benchmarking performance and disseminating best practices, the Global Information Technology Report series . . . assesses the progress of networked readiness in countries, revealing the obstacles that prevent countries from fully capturing the benefits of ICT. Beyond just providing a yearly "snapshot" of networked readiness . . . we want to . . . establish a process whereby governments, businesses and other stakeholders can evaluate progress on a continual basis.[36]

According to former Forum CEO Jose-Maria Figueres, the reports also serve to disseminate information in developing countries about the potential of ICT, promote better leadership dedicated to improving global connectivity, and, importantly, to promote competition between countries in making ICT provision better and more extensive.[37]

The 2003–4 edition of the *GITR*, the third in the series, bears the subtitle "Towards an Equitable Information Society." In the introduction, Figueres identifies the main challenge in ICT as how to provide connectivity and empowerment to the 5 billion people who are not the well-off consumers of the developed world. He poses the question whether the best way to empower the global poor is to provide the latest versions of technology, or whether it would be more practical and affordable to distribute less powerful technologies more rapidly and more widely. Figueres calls for the replication of the micro-credit model used successfully by enterprises such as the Grameen Bank to promote entrepreneurship in ICT in developing countries.[38] Again like the *GCR*, the *GITR* is divided into three parts: scholarly essays, individual country profiles, and statistical data and methodological discussion. The essayists approach the central problematic of advancing networked readiness and usage from the core Forum perspective of different stakeholders: in this case, individuals, businesses, and governments. However, they do not break out other groups of stakeholders that might have relevant and distinct perspectives, such as civil society organizations.

The scholarly articles in the 2003–4 *GITR* support the Forum's overall agenda of promoting a multi-stakeholder approach to global problem solving and building on the synergies between technology, economic growth and development. One article champions the success of Finland, a small economy with no natural advantages in ICTs, at becoming a world leader in wireless technology in the 1990s as a model for policymakers elsewhere.[39] The article by Bruno Lanvin and Christine Zhen-Wei Qiang, both of the World Bank, discussing the relationship between uptake of ICTs and the achievement of the Millennium Development Goals (MDGs) is also revealing in this regard. The authors want to make the case that investment in ICTs need not be seen as diverting resources from more pressing immediate development objectives for the poorest countries, but in fact can contribute to achieving other MDGs when the right policy mix is adopted. They construct models diagramming both direct and indirect effects that investment in what they call "e-readication" have on the eight broad Millennium Development Goals.[40]

Research and action: the Initiatives

What the Forum now calls Initiatives grew more or less organically out of the Forum's research agenda that began with projects like the Global Competitiveness Programme. Unlike the projects that produce annual research reports, most of what the Forum calls Initiatives are fixed term undertakings that have set objectives. Broadly speaking, the Initiatives represent a rapidly growing laboratory for new, hands-on multi-stakeholder undertakings to solve problems and improve global governance. The Initiatives are polymorphous: they do not have a standard form, structure, objective, timetable, set of objectives, mechanism of governance or evaluation. They probably have three general shared characteristics: they all involve public-private partnerships; they all embrace a multi-stakeholder approach to achieving their goal; and they all involve the Forum in some sort of a catalytic or enabling role, although in many cases the Forum does not take a lead role in managing Initiatives. Managing Director Richard Samans sees the Forum as functioning as a hub to connect private sector actors to governments and multilateral organizations.[41] Collectively the Initiatives are striving to develop an effective mechanism or mechanisms for translating knowledge from research into action. Whereas the annual research reports provide information and analysis to the Forum's members and the general public without specifically prescribing how it is to be used, many of the Initiatives seek to achieve specific change objectives in narrow fields, such as using technology to improve the education system of Jordan (see below). Many of the Initiatives are envisioned as experiments, in that whilst each is engineered with every intention of success, the Forum and its partners are willing and able to try new, untested approaches in the hope of solving a problem. They are also willing, as Managing Director Ged Davis commented, to pull the plug on Initiatives that do not pan out.[42] Box 5.2 lists the Forum's active Initiatives at the end of 2005.

The Initiatives vary across many dimensions: some are driven primarily by the private sector and are primarily action-oriented and charitable, whilst others may be much more intergovernmental and intellectual in focus. The Disaster Resource Network is a particularly good example of the former. Following the January 2001 Gujarat earthquake, which took place during the Davos Annual Meeting that year, Forum member firms in the construction, engineering and logistics industries organized a coordinating network to facilitate donations of goods, services and skills by the private sector to disaster relief and recovery efforts in developing countries. The DRN, now established as a freestanding not-for-profit charitable foundation in Switzerland, liaises and coordinates with the United Nations, national and local governments, and international relief agencies to ensure the most rapid and effective private sector participation following disasters.[43] An interesting example of the latter type of Initiative is the International

Box 5.2 The World Economic Forum's active initiatives at the end of 2005

Corporate Citizenship
Partnering Against Corruption
International Monetary Convention Project
Disaster Resource Network
Energy Poverty Action
Financing for Development
Global Competitiveness
Global Education Initiative
Global Governance
Global Health Initiative
Global Risk Network
Greenhouse Gas Register
India and the World Scenarios
IT Access for Everyone
Water
West-Islamic World Dialogue

Source: World Economic Forum.

Monetary Convention Project, launched in 2004, in which the Forum is providing a venue for finance ministry and central bank staffs of the leading economies to meet with business leaders and academics informally in a series of roundtable discussions about proposed reforms to the international monetary system. Research papers contributed by major academic economists, such as Robert Skidelsky, Bradford DeLong and Barry Eichengreen, are being presented at the roundtables to support debate over the thorny questions of whether the Bretton Woods system of fixed exchange rates succeeded or failed, whether it should be restored, and what should become of institutions originally established to sustain it, such as the International Monetary Fund. At the end of 2006 the project is scheduled to culminate in the publication of a report summarizing the findings of the roundtables and containing some of the research papers presented.[44] The two sections that follow provide a more in-depth look at two Initiatives that vary across yet other dimensions: the Agricultural Trade Task Force and the Jordan Education Initiative.

Supporting the WTO trade liberalization process: the Agricultural Trade Task Force

One of the major achievements of the Forum's Initiatives has been to institutionalize cooperation between the Forum and its members and other multilateral economic institutions, such as the World Trade Organization. Serving as a venue for Track II diplomacy, the Forum has provided a channel for stakeholders in multilateral trade liberalization negotiations to understand and articulate their interests and, through formation of alliances of interest, to maximize their leverage upon the official parties to the Track I negotiations: the nation-state government members of the WTO. One of the important aspects of the Forum's involvement in the WTO's Doha Development Round is that the Forum has been a key player in developing and strengthening business associations in developing countries through its regional dialogues and summits. Traditionally firms in developing countries have had less well organized, less effective business associations than their counterparts in industrial nations, with the resulting effect that they have been less effective in assuring that their governments have represented their interests properly in multilateral trade rounds. Arguably, Forum activities have been reducing the disparity between the ability of firms and industries in the industrial world and firms and industries in developing countries to organize and represent themselves in multilateral trade negotiations.

The Forum took a major step in aligning the interests of its member firms with the trade liberalization agenda of the WTO's Doha Development Round by creating an Agricultural Trade Task Force that engaged in dialogue on the problems facing the lifting of barriers to agricultural trade, and issued a communiqué of recommendations in June 2003 strongly endorsing agricultural trade liberalization as an engine of economic development for poor countries. Comprised of Forum member firms such as Nestle SA and General Mills Inc., CSOs such as CARE International and CAFOD (Catholic Agency for Overseas Development), multilateral institutions such as the World Bank, industry and consumer alliances such as the Confederation of Indian Industry and Consumers International, the makeup of the Forum's Agricultural Trade Task Force epitomized Klaus Schwab's multi-stakeholder approach to global problem solving.[45] Membership of the Task Force united different types of actors based in industrial and developing countries around a project of constructing a shared perspective on the importance of agricultural trade liberalization to economic development.

The Agricultural Trade Task Force's communiqué was issued in the runup to the WTO Cancun ministerial meeting expressly to bring pressure upon delegates to Cancun to make liberalizing concessions: "The World Economic Forum Agricultural Trade Task Force . . . reiterates is urgent call for decisive and comprehensive action by trade and international development ministers participating in the forthcoming Cancun Ministerial of the WTO."[46] The communiqué was an important declaration of a transnational alliance of global business interests and elements of the traditional economic development community favouring the liberalization of agricultural trade. Hence the first significant achievement recorded in the Task Force's communiqué was the alignment of the interests of Forum member firms with the poverty reduction objectives of multilateral organizations, CSOs and developing country governments. By assenting to the main objective of the Task Force's report being poverty reduction, large global firms on the Task Force, such as Kraft Foods, Coca Cola and Unilever, were acknowledging that their own traditionally understood material interests as firms, such as increasing profits, market share, return on investment and increasing the stock price, would be best served by embracing and sharing a global poverty reduction agenda with the types of actors in the development community who also had once viewed the interests of global firms and civil society as much more oppositional. Citing a 2001 World Bank report, the communiqué argues that "the total benefit of liberalizing agricultural trade globally should be in the region of US$250 billion by 2015, of which almost $150 billion would accrue to developing countries."[47] The Task Force constructed poverty reduction across the developing world as a positive-sum project that could be expected to benefit the poor in developing countries and also global firms in the agriculture and food industries.

The Task Force outlined three broad tactical objectives to further the achievement of its strategic objective of poverty reduction: equitable trade policies; creating stronger agricultural producers in developing countries; and consideration of social concerns. Under equitable trade policies fall the Task Force's main priorities for the Doha Round: "market-distorting export subsidies, export credits and direct payments, as well as market access restrictions (especially tariff escalation and peak tariffs) in developed countries place particularly damaging limitations on economic growth potential in developing countries and should be eliminated."[48] The main obstacles to agricultural trade liberalization that the Task Force identified come from government: US and EU agricultural policies. Hence

firms, business associations, multilateral institutions and development CSOs, by aligning behind a liberalization agenda, hoped to
alter the balance of political pressure upon US and EU policymakers at Cancun specifically and throughout the remainder of the
Doha round.

However, by linking equitable trade policies to stronger producers in
developing countries and consideration of social concerns as tactical
objectives, the Task Force communiqué makes demands upon a wide
range of actors to undertake reforms, therein avoiding the construction
of a polarization of interests assigning blame and obligations to
reform to governments alone. To strengthen agricultural producers in
developing countries, the report calls for multilateral institutions such
as the World Bank and other private donors to reverse the twenty-year
decline in rural development aid and calls for land reform and
improved access to credit for rural producers. Under consideration of
social concerns, the alliance represented by the Task Force endorses
derogation from the neoliberal, one-size-fits-all model of trade liberalization for developing countries' agricultural sectors:

> the goal is the dynamic, long term development of an open and
> fair and equitable trading system, but developing countries should
> also have the flexibility to support and protect low-income and
> resource-poor producers of staple crops from overwhelming
> competition that threatens their livelihood and undermines their
> security.[49]

This position is significant, in that a more materialist understanding
of business interests would expect global firms to favour complete
trade liberalization unless they could realize specific material gains
through sectoral protection, in which case they would be expected to
use legislative and regulatory processes to seek economic rents. By
participating in the discourse structured by the World Economic
Forum, firms in the global food industry have come to see raising the
living standards of the global poor, and thus their potential to
become greater producers and consumers, as a priority approach to
"growing the business." The Task Force's final recommendation
captured the positive-sum, mutual interest-based need for action: "It
is incumbent upon companies, donor and local governments, and
non-governmental agencies alike to evaluate their own practices and
engage in a constructive agricultural trade reform and capacity-
building process based on partnership, shared goals and mutual
respect."[50]

The Jordan Education Initiative

The Jordan Education Initiative (JEI) is a particularly useful window through which to view the Forum's Initiatives for several reasons: it involves a substantial range of public and private partners; it has already achieved identifiable accomplishments, and yet is ongoing; clear criteria have been established and applied to measure its accomplishments; and the Forum is attempting to replicate its model elsewhere. The JEI was born out of discussions that took place at an Industry Governors' meeting of the information and communications technology sector at the 2003 Davos Annual Meeting. Business leaders in the ICT sector wanted to create a public-private partnership to demonstrate how ICTs could be placed at the core of a programme to revitalize primary and secondary education in such a way as to stimulate economic development and growth. With remarkable speed, a programme was developed, and, at the suggestion of Cisco CEO John Chambers, the government of the Hashemite Kingdom of Jordan agreed for Jordan to be the test country. The Forum signed up Forum members Cisco Systems and Computer Associates (CA), already Strategic Partners of the Forum, to serve as Initiative Partners and take the lead role in global private sector participation. Three main objectives were set for the JEI: (1) develop and implement subject e-curricula, first in mathematics and then in other subjects, place the latest educational technologies in all classrooms and train teachers how to use them; (2) adapt e-curricula and educational technologies for use in creating a lifelong learning system to serve the vocational and broader educational needs of adult Jordanians; and (3) develop the Jordanian ICT industry through public-private partnerships to support education in Jordan. A fourth objective that emerged, as the JEI got off the ground, was to generate a model for technology-infused education reform that could be transferred to other countries.[51]

The JEI was launched formally in June 2003 at an "extraordinary meeting" of the Forum at the Dead Sea in Jordan, only six months after its inception, following intensive preparatory work by the World Economic Forum, the Jordanian government and the two Initiative Partners, Cisco and CA. A total of thirty-four partners were signed up to participate, of which twenty-two were from the private sector, four were from the public sector, seven were civil society organizations (including charitable foundations), and one was a university. Of the total, nineteen partners were global and fifteen were Jordanian. Each global partner was paired with a local counterpart, facilitating local accountability and also promoting knowledge and capacity transfer to the Jordanian partners. As the JEI progressed, the local partners were able to take on more responsibilities for execution and delivery. The work of the partners was to be coordinated by a small Project Management Office organized by the Forum and funded by Cisco, CA, Microsoft and the Jordanian Ministry of ICT, with three tiers of governing bodies that would meet periodically to supervise and manage the overall direction of the project. Commitments of funding were rapid and extensive. By February 2005, US\$22 million in funds, technology and labour had been contributed, of which 50 percent was supplied by the global private sector, 32 percent by international donors (of which the US Agency for International Development, the US Middle East Partnership Initiative and the British Council were the largest), 11 percent by the Jordanian government, 6 percent from the Jordanian private sector and 1 percent from CSOs, universities and charitable foundations.[52]

The next, developmental phase of the initiative involved hiring staff for the Project Management Office, developing and pre-testing an e-curriculum for mathematics, and engaging partners to develop e-curricula for other subjects. Completed in just fourteen months, by September 2004 the first part of the programme was ready to be rolled out in a group of twelve selected pilot schools in Amman, which were called "Discovery" schools. The mathematics e-curriculum was introduced, projectors and other technologies were delivered to the schools, "math labs" were installed in schools, and teachers and principals received training in the new technologies. In the spring of 2005 e-curricula for science, English as a foreign language, and ICT began to be tested, with Arabic due to be introduced in early 2006. By September 2005 the number of Discovery schools was to rise to 100, with the intention eventually to spread the new e-curricula, technology and teacher training to all Jordanian schools. The Jordanian ICT industry has developed substantially, although largely through the direct transfer of knowledge and capacity from global partners in developing e-curricula, rather than in ways that the JEI originally envisaged. Most interestingly, from late 2004, even as the e-curricula had barely been launched, the publicity the JEI received led to requests from over ten countries in the Middle East and elsewhere to adapt the programme to their needs. The Forum responded by undertaking initiatives replicating the JEI in Rajasthan in India and in Palestine, thereby placing the Jordan Education Initiative under a the tent of a broadened Global Education Initiative.[53]

The Jordan Education Initiative has benefited from having both its accomplishments and weaknesses documented externally, both so that the programme can be improved as it progresses and so that subsequent initiatives elsewhere will function better from the start. The global consultants McKinsey & Company, working with Jordanian consulting firm RazorView, studied the development and implementation of the JEI intensively on a *pro bono* basis and produced a detailed report in February 2005. The report recounts a concise history of the JEI and then analyzes the specific outputs of the programme and the broader outcomes achieved for the partners, for Jordan, and for global development in general. The McKinsey study found that up to that point the development of e-curricula had been most successful, with notable but less complete successes in deploying technology in classrooms, teacher training, and developing the Jordanian ICT industry. Only the lifelong learning programme had failed to get off the ground properly. Based on their findings, McKinsey came up with a set of seven recommendations for realizing successful global-local, public-private partnerships, ranging from locating projects in countries with attractive governmental, social and geo-strategic conditions to assigning programme activities so as best to leverage appropriate partner competences.[54] (See Box 5.3).

The early successes of the Jordan Education Initiative, incomplete though they may be, as evaluated by the McKinsey report are enor-

---

Box 5.3 McKinsey & Company's recommendations for realizing successful global-local, public-private partnerships

1 Attractive governmental, social and geo-strategic conditions
2 Clear vision and objectives, powerfully articulated in appropriate forums
3 Motivated partners, whose interests are aligned with initiative, providing sufficient inputs
4 Programme activities that leverage appropriate partner competences
5 Well supported coordinating mechanisms
6 Consistent monitoring and evaluation
7 Effective governance to set strategic direction and align partners.

Source: McKinsey & Company, "Building Effective Public-Private Partnerships: Lessons Learnt from the Jordan Education Initiative" (2005), 12–14.

mously important for the World Economic Forum as it develops its research programme, its Initiatives, and in particular the role that the Forum wants to develop of serving as a catalyst for multi-stakeholder public-private partnerships. The JEI has virtually all the elements that the Forum is seeking to achieve its "entrepreneurship in the global public interest," "committed to improving the state of the world" mission: a pragmatic project driven by a strong vision that brings together private and public partners, global and local resources, using the latest technologies, to help build civil society, bring about real social change, and also create value for investors and shareholders and other stakeholders in the private sector. Most importantly, the successful model of the JEI should be replicable, not only to other countries and localities, but also to other social fields, such as delivery of healthcare. The main challenge it will face as it is replicated is scalability: whilst private sector resources may be forthcoming for a small country such as Jordan, undertaking a similar initiative in a large country such as Bangladesh or the Democratic Republic of Congo might be so daunting as to fail to attract private partners. Such initiatives will need to rely upon clearly demonstrated successes in order to attract continuing interest from existing and potential new partners in propagating them farther afield.

6   Engaging the critics

Introduction: existential and instrumental critics

This chapter seeks to understand the principal types of criticisms of the World Economic Forum, by whom they have been made, and how the Forum has responded. The story that emerges is one of learning and adaptation, both by the Forum and by its critics, and of fluid and shifting boundaries between those driving the Forum's agenda and those seeking to change it. The actual narrative of the Forum's engagement with its critics challenges the oppositionalism constructed by those who embrace the "Shar-pei" and "Wolf in Sheep's Clothing" narratives of the Forum's evolution. This story sets the Forum somewhat apart from large multilateral economic institutions such as the WTO, World Bank and IMF, which have had more fixed boundaries and identities that are tied more directly to economic policies that tend to engender clearly staked out ideological opposition.

The critics of the World Economic Forum can be divided broadly into two levels: those who question the Forum at an existential level – its mission, its membership, its methods of operation – and those who criticize it at an instrumental level, arguing that the Forum is not doing what it intends to do as well as it might or ought to do. The existential critics tend to come from segments of global civil society that challenge the socioeconomic configuration of globalization as at its core neoliberal and inherently unjust, and they tend to view the Forum as an instrument of neoliberal globalization through the discourse that it constructs and drives. The instrumental critics are sympathetic to the broad aims and objectives of the Forum, and often tend to be present or former members of the Forum itself. The Forum has had its instrumental critics since its inception in the 1970s, whereas the existential critics only turned their focus upon the Forum as a result of the Forum's own remarkably effective publicity in the 1990s. In some ways, the instrumental critiques can be seen as extensions of internal debates within different constituents of the Forum about its objectives and means of achieving them. In what initially might appear surprising, in the 2000s the Forum appears to have had relatively greater success at addressing the concerns of the existential critics than those of the instrumental critics. Two broad sets of criticisms can be regarded as existential. First and foremost is the argument that the Forum's agenda and discourse are inherently neoliberal and thus benefit the Forum's corporate members at the expense of the rest of civil society. The second set of arguments is that Forum's public diplomacy serves to conceal its private functions of serving members through providing a venue for private dealmaking and facilitating access to public policy-makers; and that core elements of the Forum's activities, such as its not-for-profit status, are more ambiguous than they appear and thus raise serious ethical questions that need to be addressed. Most other criticisms can be treated as instrumental, two of which will be discussed in the sections that follow: the question of the Forum's size and content mix, and issues relating to management style and effectiveness.

Contested terrain, shifting discourse

By far the most serious existential critique of the Forum is the basic challenge to its agenda and discourse. Many intellectuals of the traditional left would regard the World Economic Forum as a manifestation of a Gramscian historic bloc, at the core of which economic interests organized around manufacturing and finance capital are joined to ideas and policy.[1] In the 1930s the Italian Marxist scholar Antonio Gramsci argued that leading social groups or classes representing the dominant mode of production form governing alliances, known as historic blocs, with other social groups in order to secure sufficient consent of the governed to maintain order and social peace. Leading groups, according to Gramsci, use ideologies, such as nationalism, and culture to persuade other social groups to participate in the historic bloc. They are able to achieve their objective through a process known as *trasformismo*, wherein they make concessions in terms of distribution of economic goods and power that are sufficient to ensure other groups' consent in the leading group's governance but do not threaten the leading group's hold over power.[2] For neo-Gramscian scholars in the 1990s, the rise of an opposition to neoliberal globalization linked across national boundaries raised the possibility that technology has changed global society in such a way that a transnational counter-hegemonic project may have become feasible.[3] Whether the experience of challenging the Forum reinforces such an oppositional view of social hegemonies or not will become evident in the discussion that follows.

The opposition to the Forum and its Davos Annual Meetings that became visible in the late 1990s was comprised of much the same red-green-brown populist coalition that opposed the signing of the Treaty of Marrakech in 1995, the creation of and US membership in the World Trade Organization, the ongoing activities of the World Bank, International Monetary Fund and other multilateral financial institutions in the late 1990s, and the proposed Multilateral Agreement on Investment (MAI) in 1998. Deibert characterizes the coalition as "a cross-national network of citizen activists linked by electronic mailing lists and World-Wide Web home pages that vibrate with activity monitoring the global political economy like a virtual watchdog."[4] Nationalist and ruralist organizations such as the French Confédération Paysanne Française (CPF) joined with Swiss civil society organizations such as the Berne Declaration, leftist coalitions such as the Anti-WTO Coordination Switzerland (so titled in English) and transnational environmental groupings such as Friends of the Earth. Coinciding with the opening of the January 1998 Davos summit, an umbrella grouping of 192 organizations from fifty-four countries reporting an aggregate membership of 20 million and titling itself People's Global Action Against "Free" Trade and the WTO, issued a manifesto called "Declaration Against the Globalisers of Misery." The manifesto criticized the centralization of political and economic power brought about by economic globalization and its shift to undemocratic and unaccountable institutions, such as the WTO, and criticized the growth in influence of "informal" business groupings such as the Forum. People's Global Action held its own weeklong conference in Geneva attended by 600 participants a fortnight after the 1998 Davos summit. Seminars and roundtables on the WTO, the MAI, food production, culture and economics were followed by small group meetings to plan how to leverage the knowledge shared and gained at the conference. The organization held a meeting on 27 February 1998 to kick off a pan-European civil disobedience movement against free trade.[5]

Opponents of the Forum used the internet extensively and successfully to organize a protest against the 2000 Davos Annual Meeting, much as they had done to mobilize popular support against the MAI in 1998. In essence, the MAI had been the catalyst for the emergence of the alter-globalization movement as a viable social force through cyberspace. The MAI was a proposed treaty being negotiated under the auspices of the Organization for Economic Cooperation and Development that would have instituted a broad, neoliberal regime committed to dismantling barriers to flows of foreign direct investment (FDI). A diverse alliance of CSOs and developing country governments came together to oppose the MAI primarily on the grounds that transnational firms might be able to use the treaty to challenge any existing social legislation in signatory countries, such as labor and environmental protections, on the grounds that it disadvantaged potential foreign investors. Opponents of the MAI also claimed that nation-state governments were working with global firms through the OECD to negotiate it in relative secrecy, without the participation of civil society, with the intention of presenting it once completed as a *fait accompli*. Relying upon the internet as the primary channel of communication, MAI opponents were able to inform the global public of their view of the impending treaty and make its adoption sufficiently unpalatable politically to OECD member governments as to convince the OECD to postpone further work on the treaty indefinitely. The three main functions of the internet identified by Deibert as crucial to organizing opposition to the MAI were employed in opposing the Forum as well: communicating information swiftly amongst members, publicizing information about the organization to the internet-using public and beyond, and applying direct pressure upon politicians and policymakers.[6]

Box 6.1 lists organizations and alliances that have been active in criticizing the World Economic Forum.

Box 6.1 Partial list of organizations and alliances that have been active as critics of the World Economic Forum

- Anti-WTO Coordination Switzerland
- Association of Brazilian NGOs
- Berne Declaration
- Confédération paysanne française
- Friends of the Earth
- Globalization Challenge Initiative
- Greenpeace
- People's Global Action Against "Free" Trade and the WTO
- "Public Eye on Davos" project
- World Social Forum

The text of a leaflet summoning protesters to Davos, authored by Alain Kessi of Anti-WTO Coordination Switzerland and dated 25 December 1999 (translated from German to English), appearing on the World Wide Web, offers a concise characterization of how the opposition to the Forum's version of globalization viewed the Forum and how it perceived the role and achievements of its own counter-hegemonic project.[7] In the leaflet Kessi tracks the rise in importance of the Forum: "When it was founded in 1971 the (Forum) was but a management seminar among others. By now it has become one of the most important 'think tanks' of the economic strategists of the North." Concurring with the Forum's own claim, Kessi credited the Forum with getting the GATT Uruguay round launched and warned that, after protesters had succeeded in derailing the launch of a new GATT millennium round in Seattle, the Forum was planning to use the Davos summit to revive a new multilateral GATT round. Critiquing the Forum's own publicity, Kessi contrasts the Forum's themes for the public and private faces of the 1999 Davos summit. On the same day that Klaus Schwab promoted the summit's 1999 theme of humanizing globalization through addressing social and environmental issues, with large advertisements in Swiss newspapers, Kessi asserts, Chevron President Richard Matke and Russian Federation Prime Minister Yevgeny Primakov met privately in Davos to settle a long-running dispute between Turkey and Russia over the route of certain oil pipelines and simultaneously to plan the arrest of Kurdish Workers Party (PKK) leader Abdullah Ocalan.[8]

In the event, the protest at the 2000 Davos Annual Meeting attracted over 2000 protesters, who marched on the Centre des Congrès whilst President Clinton was speaking. Blocked from reaching the meeting by significant numbers of police in riot gear, the protesters trashed a McDonald's, a close-at-hand symbol of the type of globalization they were criticizing.[9] For the first time, the Davos summit had to be defended by the Swiss Federal Police. Jose Bové, head of the Confédération Paysanne Française and one of the leaders of the protest, attacked the Forum for the dual-channel public and private nature of its meetings, arguing that it was improper for leaders of transnational firms and governments to have a private, back channel venue for taking decisions affecting the public interest and that it was improper for business leaders to assume roles analogous to political leaders in international relations.[10] Bové, in consultation with the CPF and the Anti-WTO Coordination, rejected on principle an invitation from the Forum to participate in the Annual Meeting and expressed the fear that multilateral trade negotiations aborted at Seattle could resume at Davos.[11]

Other protesting organizations, however, saw value in articulating their views inside the Davos summit as well as outside, and the Forum welcomed their participation. During the 2000 Davos summit, three NGOs – the Berne Declaration, Friends of the Earth, and the Globalization Challenge Initiative – announced the launch of a jointly run ongoing project entitled Public Eye on Davos, which would monitor the Forum and challenge it both from within and from without, questioning "the legitimacy of a private event which influences international politics" and disseminating information about the activities and positions of CSOs.[12] The Public Eye on Davos project invited CSO representatives Vandana Shiva of the Third World Network and Manuel Chiriboga of the Asociacion Latinoamericana de Organizaciones de Promocion, to take part with Forum Chairman Klaus Schwab and Goran Lindahl of the construction firm ABB in a Davos panel on CSOs and the Forum on 28 January 2000.

The process of counter-organizing had advanced by the time of the 2001 Annual Meeting. CSO concern focused on the unaccountability of Forum-promoted intensification of relations between the United Nations and the private sector under a "Global Compact" backed by UN Secretary General Kofi Annan. In December 2000 CSOs monitoring the Forum called upon the United Nations and global business leaders to endorse a "Citizens' Compact" backed by over seventy CSOs that would mandate the UN, as a more democratically accountable multilateral body than the Forum, to develop a legal framework to monitor and govern the behaviour of global firms.[13] Various alternative summits were convened simultaneously with the Forum, including a conference open to the public in Davos itself, hosted by the Public Eye on Davos project, which was intended to articulate a critical perspective on the Forum and its agenda by focusing on four topics: global governance, international trade politics, international financial relations and corporate control.[14] This movement has evolved into an annual Public Eye on Davos Awards presentation by the Swiss CSOs Pro Natura-Friends of the Earth and the Berne Declaration simultaneously with the Forum's Annual Meeting in Davos. The awards are intended to name and shame large transnational firms that the organizers seek to publicize as particular exemplars of corporate social and environmental irresponsibility.[15]

More dramatically, an alternative organization, entitled the World Social Forum to parallel the World Economic Forum, was created by a group of civil society organizations to promote a counter-hegemonic, alternative version of globalization simultaneously with the World Economic Forum's Davos meeting. The first annual meeting of the

World Social Forum was convened in Porto Alegre, Brazil at the end of January 2001, bringing together several thousand representatives of civil society organizations and other participants to debate and publicize ideas to advance sustainable development, social justice and human rights, and further to democratize international organizations. Jose Bové, a leader of the protests at Davos in 2000, took a leading role as a presenter at the World Social Forum summit in 2001.[16] During the first World Social Forum meeting Bové participated in a raid on a farm near Porto Alegre owned by the global agribusiness firm Monsanto, in which experimental genetically modified crops were uprooted. The World Social Forum grew rapidly as a movement and as an annual, rival event to the Davos annual meeting. The 2005 World Social Forum annual meeting in Porto Alegre drew more than 100,000 participants from over 2000 organizations and from at least 119 countries. Over 2000 debates and other events took place, loosely organized around eleven themes, including land reform, human rights, climate change, and "ethics, cosmo-visions and spiritualities."[17]

Yet the perceived successes of the World Social Forum in broadening public debate over how the global economy should be organized, and in getting many of their agenda items included in the discussions at Davos, has raised significant questions for World Social Forum organizers about their organization's future. Some organizers argue that the World Social Forum has achieved its principal objectives, and that its members should focus their energies on pressing their agenda at Davos, whilst others contend that there remains a need for the World Social Forum to raise public consciousness of their agenda from outside the World Economic Forum. According to UN Millennium Development Goals Campaign director Salis Shetty, "slowly Davos is starting to increase its involvement in these issues, but the Social Forum remains an important source of pressure."[18] Brazilian President Inácio Lula da Silva, elected with massive support from critics of the impact of neoliberal globalization on Brazil's poor, addressed the annual meetings of both the World Social Forum and the World Economic Forum in 2005. He displeased some of his more radical populist supporters at Porto Alegre by his decision to go to Davos, but in the process underscored the necessity of taking the Porto Alegre agenda to the Davos participants. Lula da Silva's strategy revealed one of the weaknesses of the World Social Forum as a venue for global problem solving: whilst attracting and accommodating much larger numbers of participants than the World Economic Forum, the World Social Forum has attracted a relatively less diverse range of participants, both in terms of ideological perspective and in terms of their respective institutional capacities for action, than the range of organizations in attendance at Davos.

The important story to emerge from this flowering of engagement by civil society has been the extent to which the World Economic Forum has engaged the critics of its agenda and discourse. Most significantly, the Forum took the criticism seriously from the start. In the view of Klaus Schwab and the managing directors, the multi-stakeholder approach to problem solving and global governance that has been a hallmark of the Forum has always intended to be inclusive of civil society as a stakeholder. What the protests and formation of the World Social Forum brought home to the World Economic Forum was that they had thitherto not done a sufficiently good job of communicating the opportunities and channels for participation, and that they needed to take a more proactive approach to broadening participation of civil society organizations and other stakeholders across global civil society, including the global public itself. Beginning at the 2003 Annual Meeting, the World Economic Forum began co-hosting the Davos "Open Forum" with the Federation of Swiss Protestant Churches during the Annual meeting. The Open Forum, held in a 300-seat Davos school auditorium, features a series of debates open to the public on major social, political and economic topics being discussed by the delegates to the Annual Meeting. Each Open Forum is co-sponsored by a major civil society organization, is moderated by a leading media figure, and features major participants from across the range of Forum members and communities attending Davos.[19]

The World Economic Forum also increased its invitations to civil society organizations to participate in Davos and other Forum meetings, including organizations that were active at the World Social Forum. Amnesty International, for example, delivered the same message about values for globalization in January 2003 to the World Economic Forum at Davos and the World Social Forum at Porto Alegre: "Globalise respect for human rights, globalise justice and globalise accountability for those who abuse rights."[20] As the global discourse shifted and the two organizations evolved, with numerous civil society organizations participating in both annual meetings, a dialogue emerged in which different points of view could be debated without extreme ideological polarization. At Davos in January 2003, Klaus Schwab told Inter Press News Service, "I have just one word to Porto Alegre – we are the same. Both events, in principle, have the same objectives. That is to create a better world."[21] When asked whether the thinking processes of the World Economic Forum and World Social Forum could converge to create a visionary platform,

Schwab replied that both forums were trying to achieve the same objective, but whereas the World Social Forum was tied to a specific philosophy, the World Economic Forum was not. He welcomed dialogue between the two Forums as long as it was about learning from each other and not about one side only wanting to convince the other of their rightness.[22]

Keenly interested in the World Social Forum, World Economic Forum Managing Director and COO André Schneider was scheduled to participate in a debate with three World Social Forum members in Paris in the summer of 2005. Schneider is swift to emphasize that the World Economic Forum welcomes dialogue with all organizations that are willing to engage in a civil manner. In the early 2000s the Forum had a well publicized disagreement with Greenpeace, which had brought its campaign against global warming to the 2001 Davos Annual Meeting. According to Schneider, the World Economic Forum and Greenpeace were in the process of writing a statement that both sides agreed would remain private until it was ready for public release. The day after the embargo agreement was made, Greenpeace released the statement to the public, and when the Forum criticized it for doing so, Greenpeace responded that the Forum was trying to silence it. This, Schneider recounts, resulted in Greenpeace not being invited back to Davos the following year.[23] One measure of the World Economic Forum's success in engaging discursively with its critics and their agendas is the extent to which critics have acknowledged it openly. Fatima Melo, a representative of the Association of Brazilian NGOs and an organizer of the World Social Forum's 2005 Porto Alegre meeting, told the BBC, "many of our approaches have been incorporated by Davos and by institutions like the World Bank."[24] The Forum's efforts to broaden the participation of civil society organizations was by some measures so successful that at the end of the 2005 Annual Meeting, which focused extensively on poverty reduction and global climate change, the Confederation of British Industry's Director General Sir Digby Jones complained publicly that these organizations had "hijacked" the Forum and were forcing business to apologize for itself.[25]

The Forum also took institutional steps to incorporate the social agenda of its critics. One such undertaking was a major project to increase the participation of women in Forum activities and to address global issues of particular concern to women. In 2001 the Forum established the Women Leaders Programme to focus attention on the global conditions of women, the role of women in society and women in leadership roles. Headed by Marilyn Carlson Nelson, Chair and

CEO of Carlson Companies, a major privately held American marketing, travel and hospitality firm, the Women Leaders Programme holds seminars and panel discussions at Forum events around the globe and commissions economic research into the conditions of women. By the end of 2005 over thirty seminars and panels had been held. In autumn 2005 the Women Leaders Programme and the Forum's Global Competitiveness Programme released a major research report, "Women's Empowerment: Measuring the Global Gender Gap," which quantifies and measures the impact of the lack of utilization of the economic resources and power of women upon the competitiveness of nation-states. The study measures the extent to which women in fifty-eight countries have achieved equality with men in terms of economic participation, economic opportunity, political empowerment, educational attainment, and health and well-being. The report, drawn from public data from international organizations and national statistics and from the Forum's Executive Opinion Survey, is intended to serve as a benchmark of best practices as well as weaknesses, and to promote policy transfer from more successful to less successful nation-states.[26] The Women Leaders Programme also claims credit for increasing the participation of women at the Davos Annual Meeting from 8 percent to 15 percent between 2002 and 2005, and increasing the percentage of women panelists at Davos from 9 percent to 13 percent over the same period.[27] In an absolute sense those figures are not dramatic, but they perhaps assume greater significance when one takes in the continuing under-representation of women in senior management of global business.

Ethical issues: public vs. private, profit vs. not-for-profit

Existential critics of the World Economic Forum have continued to contend at a general level that that the Forum's public debates and projects conceal its private functions as a network providing business leaders access to public policymakers and as a private venue for business dealmaking – the "Wolf in Sheep's Clothing" narrative. This contention is essentially an ethical claim, and one of a dual nature. The basis for the first part of the claim, that the Forum is somehow being deceptive, probably arose as a result of the effectiveness of the Forum's public diplomacy in telling the story of its public agenda and activities. The interaction between the Forum's members and invited guests at meetings and summits is not only transparent, but widely reported by the Forum and the media. The Forum would have little reason to publicize the private deals made by its members at Forum events and venues, but lack of publicity hardly equates to an intent to deceive. The basis for the second part of the claim, that there is something improper about the Forum's public and private functions taking place simultaneously, and even that there is something improper about private business deals being negotiated, is more long-running and ideological in nature. The Forum has responded to this type of criticism by being transparent to the maximum extent possible about the public side of its activities. Concerning the private side there is little that the Forum could do to respond, but given the ideological basis for the critique, it is difficult to think of a response that would be positively received, so in the end both sides are probably content to disagree on this issue.

A more concrete instance of the public vs. private criticism concerns the distinction between for-profit and not-for-profit business activities as it relates to the Forum. Another achievement of the Davos protesters was to bring to the attention of the general public a challenge to the Forum's status as a nonprofit organization by drawing attention to the links between the Forum and a series of private business ventures undertaken by Klaus Schwab and from which, according to a front-page *Wall Street Journal* article appearing at the time of the 2000 Davos summit, Schwab profited personally.[28] The *Journal* article criticized Schwab for, among other things, accepting stock options and a seat on the board of directors of San Francisco-based internet consulting firm USWeb/CKS a fortnight after the Forum had awarded USWeb/CKS an $8 million contract in 1998. Schwab told the *New York Times* he had sought to make the World Economic Forum Foundation the beneficiary of the options, but was advised by council that the board member legally had to be the holder of the options.[29] The raising of this issue highlighted again the differences between perspectives on relationships between public and private interests. Forum opponents viewed Schwab's business ventures as evidence of a conflict between the public and private faces of the Forum's information output, and of duplicity over the Forum's nonprofit status. By contrast, as online technology journal *Redherring.com* reporter Tony Perkins observed, in the Silicon Valley, New Economy business community these types of commercial relationships are considered "business as usual" and not ethically questionable.[30] Schwab, hurt by the accusations, said emphatically, "I never made one dollar based on using my privileged relationship with the forum for me personally."[31] Interrelationships between the Forum's public mission and private ventures are not uncommon, and the Forum makes no attempt to conceal them. Various ventures have been spun off of Forum ventures with member firms in the 1990s. Closer to home, in 1996 the Forum formed a joint venture, Global Event Management, with a French firm, Nephthalie, which later became Publicis Events, to manage all the logistics for Davos and other conferences.[32]

For their part, the Forum's senior management make clear that they take their commitment to the personal ethical probity of their senior officers very seriously, as is illustrated by the case of the Forum's last CEO, Jose Maria Figueres. Figueres was a major catch for the Forum's senior management when hired in the early 2000s. Holding degrees in Engineering from the US Military Academy (West Point) and Public Administration from the Kennedy School of Government at Harvard, he held senior management posts in major Central American firms in the 1980s before going on to serve as Costa Rica's Minister for Foreign Trade and Minister for Agriculture, and was subsequently elected President in 1994. Although eminently qualified and capable to manage the Forum, Figueres left the Forum in the fall of 2004 after it emerged that he had received payments as a consultant on information technology in Costa Rica after he commenced employment at the Forum, and that he had not disclosed to the Forum. Whilst not illegal, Figueres' non-disclosure of the payments violated the Forum's strict governance structure, and he took the decision to leave so as not to compromise the reputation of the Forum.[33]

Instrumental criticisms

The first group of instrumental criticisms of the Forum, which concern the size and content mix of the Davos gathering, have been ongoing and have been made largely by Forum member firms. By the early 1990s, some of the Forum's member firms were complaining about the growing size of the Annual Meeting, and, in the wake of the Forum's high visibility in shaping the post-Cold War political and economic environment, others were objecting that what they perceived to be the Forum's core focus on business and management issues had given way to too much attention to global public policy.[34] The fear was that as the number of attendees at Davos continued to grow, the intimacy and informality of the meeting would be lost, access to top decisionmakers would become more limited, and the frequency of chance meetings that would open doors to valuable networks would decline. The Forum took the decision to limit the number of attendees at Davos from the 1994 Annual Meeting, but the issue has continued to lie close to the surface, and was revived in 2002 when the number of attendees at the Annual Meeting held in New York was substantially higher. Faced with heavy criticism of the New York meeting's size, as well as the dilution of the remote, intimate environment characteristic of Davos, the Forum renewed its commitment to keep numbers limited when the Forum returned to Davos the following year. Still, at Davos some panel sessions are fully booked quickly, and some participants are now forced to stay in hotels outside of the village. Yet whilst participants may agree that the only way around the problem is for the Annual Meeting to become somewhat smaller, nobody is likely to be willing for their place to be the one that is downsized. Likewise the content question recurred in 2005, as some members criticized the Davos agenda for being too focused on issues such as poverty reduction at the expenses of "harder" business issues, resulting in a planned incremental shift of mix for the 2006 Annual Meeting. Others regard the Forum as trying to run too many panels altogether, with quantity often substituting for quality and fewer opportunities for the informal networking that so many participants still regard as the greatest value added at Davos. The Forum's staff, always listening to members and other participants, appear to be sensitive to such criticisms and seek to keep the Forum reasonably well tuned to members' interests. The issues of size and content are likely to remain near the centre of the Forum's planning process going forward.

A second group of instrumental criticisms centres around issues related to how the Forum is managed. One issue concerns how new ideas are implemented within the Forum itself. Since he started the Forum, Klaus Schwab has been a constant generator of ideas for new directions for the Forum. At times even Forum staff have expressed frustration that new ideas once proposed do not all come to fruition. Schwab himself has observed that often he has been better at strategy than operations, generating new ideas for ways to grow the Forum and its mission outside of Davos and then leaving others to implement them, assuming that they would share his same vision and sense of urgency.[35] Answering criticism that some ventures that the Forum has attempted have failed, such as WELCOM, Schwab responds that good entrepreneurship means being keen to keep trying new ideas and not being afraid that some might fail.[36] A deeper line of criticism in this vein challenges the Forum's entrepreneurial strategy of constant growth into new ventures and activities. The Forum already does too many things, and, its managers' claims notwithstanding, is too unwilling to give up on ventures that do not take off. The Forum should play to its strengths, these critics argue, by only doing things that are unique and that it is particularly qualified to do.

Another set of issues could be categorized as addressing execution at Forum events. Some complain that the quality of the regional summits is uneven. The India summit has been the best, according to one former Forum member, because of the strength of the CII within India and the importance of the Forum to the CII in maximizing its stature in the eyes of the Indian government. At a more specific level, one social entrepreneur observed that after Fair Trade had been identified as a best method for bringing about poverty reduction at the Global Town Hall meeting at Davos in 2005, subsequent sessions and workshops at the Annual Meeting did not address Fair Trade at all. Another Davos insider contended that the discussions held by the Forum of Young Global Leaders held at Zermatt in June 2005 was overly generic, allowing only 20 minutes for consideration of sweeping topics such as "world hunger." This session reportedly resulted in a press release to the effect that Young Global Leaders oppose world hunger, the impact of which was presumably open to debate. Problems of management and execution, whilst perhaps not continual, are likely to recur at the Forum, as in any other complex organization. The Forum's best tools for minimizing these difficulties are sensitivity and responsiveness.

A broader instrumental criticism that echoes one of the existential critiques is that, despite modernization of its management methods, governance of the Forum by contemporary corporate standards is still not transparent enough. The Forum continues to address this issue, for example by preparing to report its financial information according to Generally Accepted Accounting Principles (GAAP) by 2008. Further management reforms may occur following the succession of a new chief executive (see Chapter 7). Overall, the instrumental criticisms are of the sort that will persist even as the Forum continues to work to address them. The Forum has largely answered the existential criticisms to the satisfaction of many of those who would be amenable in principle to being accommodated, by, for example, being invited to participate in the Annual Meeting. Some activists still fall outside of this category. It is difficult to dissuade intellectual neo-Gramscians from their view of the Forum as acting as a sort of organic intellectual seeking to establish consensual hegemony for transnational hegemony over the globe.[37] In this perspective, at Davos meetings in the 2000s, Forum members, the Gramscian leading group, can be seen to be engaging in *trasformismo*, absorbing certain opposing interests up to a point in an attempt to co-opt opponents and thereby exercise power consensually. The difficulty that the neo-Gramscian perspective encounters is that it assumes the interests of capital and labour to be clearly distinguishable and fundamentally oppositional at the end of the day, whereas in the contemporary global economy the many different, often widely diverging interests are still less likely to be zero-sum in nature and more often than not are socially constructed. The Davos meeting and other Forum summits if anything are compelling evidence that interests can be learned, changed and reconstructed discursively through interaction with others. The Forum's multi-stakeholder approach, to the extent that it works, is intended to bring that about.

7   The Forum looking ahead

Visions of the Forum's future: a roadmap to the next level

As the World Economic Forum looks to the future midway through its fourth decade of operation, the chief developer of its strategic vision remains Klaus Schwab. The significance of Schwab's leadership role and of what he has created over thirty-five years should not be under-estimated. When introducing Professor Schwab at the 2005 India Economic Summit, Dhruv Sawhney, Chair and Managing Director of Triveni Engineering, said that Schwab had "created a United Nations of business, political and other global leaders of civil society." Schwab's name is mentioned increasingly often as a contender for the Nobel Peace Prize, indicating a broad international recognition of his skilful stewardship of a type of institution for which there was no precedent. Schwab continues to lead by articulating a clear vision of the Forum's evolving role in a changing world. Three recent texts, all or partially by Professor Schwab, indicate clearly what he sees as the main challenges facing the Forum, how he proposes to meet those challenges and where he wants the Forum to go. An internal newsletter that Schwab wrote to staff in early fall 2005 was the basis for a strategic document entitled "Roadmap 2008," which the Forum's Foundation Board approved in early November 2005. These documents reflect Schwab's vision for the Forum itself. In a presentation that he made at the India Economic Summit at the end of November 2005 to a panel session entitled "Global Challenges and India," Schwab articulated a sweeping view of ten great global challenges, how global governance can meet the challenges, and how the Forum can play a role in that governance. But Schwab's strategic vision for the Forum begs another equally important question: whither the Forum after Schwab is no longer the Forum's chief strategic architect? What has been the Forum's greatest strength becomes in another sense its greatest uncertainty looking ahead. This chapter discusses both the Forum's future in the world, as envisaged by Klaus Schwab, and the second key question facing the Forum: its future after Schwab's retirement.

The first two texts focus on how the Forum needs to grow. Schwab has always been skilled at using narrative construction to put future-oriented objectives in an historical context. In a fall 2005 internal newsletter he reflected on the evolution of the Forum's strategic objectives over its first three decades and outlined strategic objectives for the Forum in the decade 2000–10.[1] Characterizing the development of the Forum as having been "always guided by a clear strategic vision," Schwab observed that the Forum's strategic objective in its first decade, the 1970s, had been to build its reputation as the best top-level conference organizer. In the 1980s, the objective shifted to the internationalization or globalization of the Forum's activities. In the 1990s, the Forum then took on the strategic objective of building "communities" of members, strategic partners, government leaders, media and academics and others. For the decade of the 2000s, Schwab articulates a sixfold programme of strategic objectives that is intended to take the Forum to a significantly higher level of operations and involvement with its members and enable it to pursue a global agenda much more effectively:

1 Build a strong intelligence base
2 Capture the next generations of successful companies and leaders
3 Establish a physical presence in the United States and China
4 Add to the Forum's global and regional dimension a strong industry-related component
5 Put the Forum's Strategic Partners at the centre of its activities
6 Add capability for members and constituents to engage in concrete actions, particularly in the form of public-private partnerships.

In the newsletter Schwab comments on the rationale for each objective and notes considerable progress at the midpoint of the decade toward the achievement of all six. Building a stronger intelligence base, Schwab remarks, is important so that the Forum can provide members and constituents with what he calls "true strategic insights" and not be seen as primarily an organizer of conferences. This ties into concerns that Schwab has had since the 1980s about the Forum's evolving purpose, and also about public perceptions of what the Forum does. Achieving this objective requires developing the Forum's institutional capacity to provide such services and increasing the staff resources to do it. The Forum created the Centre for Strategic Insight in 2004 to be the Forum's forward-looking vehicle for identifying emerging risks and developments likely to affect Forum members and communities. Additional highly trained staff have been hired to work at Forum headquarters, with over two thirds of the 200 employees having a "top university education." The Forum, Schwab observes, is the largest employer of Harvard graduates in the Geneva area. Strategic Insight now refers not only to a particular aspect of the Forum's research output, but it is being identified and marketed as a brand within the Forum's family of research brands (Global Competitiveness, etc.). Strategic Insight research briefs are being published on Forum meetings and summits to distill the strategic insights gleaned from the dialogue, and across many Forum research products the strategic insights are being identified more clearly so as to highlight for readers the Forum's analytical value added.

The second objective, capturing the next generations of successful companies and leaders, is key if the Forum is to avoid ageing with its member firms. The composition of the Fortune 500 leading global firms is becoming progressively more dynamic and volatile, with firms entering and leaving the rankings faster than ever. Likewise the turnover rate of CEOs and senior management is accelerating. Hence to attract future leaders and growth companies as members and participants, the Forum launched the Forum of Young Global Leaders in 2004 (see Chapter 2 for more details on YGLs) and is launching a Centre for Global Growth Companies to create a community of "emerging multinationals." The Centre for Global Growth Companies is to be located in the Forum's planned office in Beijing, which at the time of writing had recently been authorized by the Chinese government, and will hold its own annual meeting.

Establishing offices in China and the United States is a strategic objective in its own right that reflects the Forum's commitment to serving the United States, its biggest nation-state constituent, better and the Forum's desire to exploit the potential for growth in Asia. Beyond the anticipated Beijing office, the Forum took the decision to locate its new Centre for Global Industries in New York in 2004 and expected the office to be open by sometime in 2006. Having a New York venue, which will include meeting facilities, also gives the Forum a physical presence close to where many member firms that are Strategic Partners or have other partnerships with the Forum are based. Creation of an industry-related component, the fourth objective, Schwab identifies as needed to enable the Forum to "become more directly relevant to the specific strategies of our partners and members." To this end, in addition to creating the Centre for Global Industries the Forum is in the process of transforming Industry Governors' meetings into Industry Partnerships. Industry Partners will have a major role in defining and furthering issues on the agenda for their respective industries. For the Forum, Industry Partnerships "represent presently the key strategic objective" because, as is noted in the Roadmap 2008 document, industry partnerships "allow the Forum to create more sustainable relationships by better penetrating [*sic*] the top management of our member companies."[2] Over the first six months of 2005, the Forum signed seventy partnership contracts and has targeted an objective of 300 such contracts by 2008 in at least ten different industries.

Schwab sees the fifth objective, putting the Forum's Strategic Partners at the centre of its activities, as necessary if the Forum hopes to be able to understand the expectations of business and multiply the Forum's knowledge and resources base. The close relationship with Strategic Partner firms that the Forum has been building over several years now offers the potential for the Forum to be able to do more "in house" through more collaborative activities with members and without having to seek outside alliances. Hence the Forum has taken the decision to "freeze" the number of Strategic Partners at 50–55 and to focus attention on deepening its relationships with this number of partners. In order to facilitate these relationships, the Forum has created a strong community management team to work directly with Strategic Partners and to report directly to Schwab as Executive Chairman.

The sixth and final objective, giving members and constituents the capacity to engage in concrete actions through public-private partnerships, is at the core of how Schwab sees the relationship of the Forum to global society as a whole. He sees this objective as about meeting global society's expectations, and cites the Forum's motto "committed to improving the state of the world" in this context. To this end the Forum created the Global Institute for Partnership and Governance, recently renamed the Centre for Public-Private Partnerships, which is running the Forum's Initiatives, several of which Schwab characterizes as "highly successful" (see Chapter 5 for more on the Initiatives). It is evident already that collectively the public-private partnerships undertaken by the Initiatives have joined the knowledge and information creation and exchange function achieved at Davos and the other Forum summits to become the Forum's second major distinctive mode of global governance. This will likely become clearer to the global public as the Initiatives expand and as the Forum's skilled public diplomacy apparatus ramps up its marketing of the Initiatives and their achievements.

The achievement of the Initiatives in institutionalizing and normalizing a mode of cross-border public-private partnerships between many different types of global and local stakeholders is hugely significant, although the Forum is not the only organizer of public-private partnerships. On one hand, as the global public comes to perceive this mode of solving public policy problems as effective, other organizations both public and private will also become more involved in coordinating such partnerships. The Forum will argue that such developments will if anything confirm that the Forum will have achieved its objective of being perceived as the best of breed, the pre-eminent "go to" group for organizing such undertakings. On the other hand, however, the impact of full publicity for the Initiatives may reveal global political cleavages over their methods and their political legitimacy, much in the way that the Forum's success at publicizing the knowledge and information creation and exchange achievements of Davos in the 1990s did. How those cleavages might manifest themselves is difficult to tell, although it is not improbable that the activities of the alter-globalization movement might serve as a template.

Envisaging the impact of the strategic objectives in the coming years, Schwab calls on the Forum staff to have a shared vision of what the Forum will be in 2008. Of five components that he enumerates, the first two are perceptual: they are about how the Forum should be seen by the rest of the world. The Forum, he says, "will be even more known as an absolutely unique international organization having considerable positive impact on the global, regional and industry agendas." Likewise, the Forum

> will be even more recognized by corporations, governments and other stakeholders of global society as an indispensable partner and catalyst for strategic insights, for innovative solutions and for collaborative efforts, always with the purpose to improving the state of the world.

These vision markers reflect the continued importance to Schwab and to the Forum's management team and staff of how the organization is seen by and known to others. In a sense the capacity to deliver goods such as strategic insights, innovative solutions to problems and collaborative efforts in problem solving is taken as given; but only to the extent that the Forum is perceived by the rest of the world, or at least ever more of it, can the Forum be able to say that it is achieving its objectives. Schwab also enumerates additional, more empirical and quantitative components of his vision for the Forum in 2008. He sees the Forum as becoming more driven by its communities, with the organization itself serving as the trustee of the Foundation's basic values: independence, integrity, quality, relevance, and service in the global public interest. This suggests an emerging process of greater self-governance, a sort of democratization of the Forum's agenda itself: a process wherein the stakeholders themselves take on a more active role in choosing how the Forum's activities and energies will be invested. Schwab sees the Forum as remaining dynamic, innovative, fast-growing and entrepreneurial, with revenues growing at a 15–20 percent annual rate to over CHF150 million by 2008/9 and staff across the three locations growing to 300.

The Forum's "Roadmap 2008" strategy document builds on the strategic vision and objectives outlined in the internal newsletter, expanding and developing some of the six objectives. Roadmap 2008 articulates eight imperatives that the Forum must undertake "to strengthen our core."

1   Reinforce our position as one of the most respected global institutions;
2   Rebalance the Annual Meeting;
3   Create and deepen community engagement;
4   Become an indispensable partner in shaping the global, regional and industry agendas;
5   Create tangible results;
6   Capture the next generations of successful companies and leaders;
7   Upgrade our organizational capabilities and prepare for risks;
8   Professionalize internal operations.

The first and most sweeping imperative is a call to excellence across all of the core aspects of the Forum's purposes and activities. This includes a commitment to being best of breed in all its undertakings and to leading by example: "we can serve our communities best by being ourselves a role model for a highly interactive, open and fast-learning community."[3] It also includes commitments to promoting its core values both internally and externally, such as promoting corporate global citizenship among its members. Management of the organization itself is a key component, through top standards of institutional governance and a collaborative, meritocratic, mentor-driven internal leadership structure. Also at the centre of the Forum's call to excellence is awareness of its "self-imposed limitations of having no official decision-making role" in global governance. The Forum is not and does not envisage becoming a legislative body. Instead, it has developed its uniquely catalytic role of bringing different stakeholders together to solve problems in an environment in which particular values, such as entrepreneurship and global public service, are already favoured. The Forum calls this the "3 Bs" approach to global problem solving: Bonding, or shared problem definition; Binding, or shared solution definition; and Building, or shared action. How the Forum is perceived by the rest of the world remains indispensable to the imperative of excellence: nurturing, developing and protecting the Forum brand identity.

The second imperative is a call essentially to keep doing what the Forum does well at Davos: to get the balance between representation and exclusivity right, to control the number of participants, to make the meeting as relevant as possible to business participants, and to strengthen the unique Davos environment of informality and bonding. The third imperative codifies the Forum's strategies for creating and developing relationships with communities of members and participants. It elaborates on objective 5 in the internal newsletter, putting Strategic Partners at the core of Forum activities, by articulating an evolving hierarchy of relationships between the Forum and the different communities. The fourth imperative elaborates on objective 4, developing Industry Partnerships to enable the Forum to become the indispensable partner for firms to shape industry agendas. The imperative also reinforces the Forum's goals of leadership in shaping regional agendas and global agendas, through strengthening the Forum's existing Global Risk Network and Global Competitiveness Network. The document envisages creating by 2008 a new Global Advisory Facility, a network that will enable teams of global leaders to provide strategic advisory services at the request of governments, international organizations and global firms on an as-needed basis. The fifth imperative reiterates objective 6 from the newsletter on the role of the Centre for Public-Private Partnerships in developing the Initiatives, and the sixth imperative reiterates objective 2 on capturing the next generation of successful firms and leaders. The seventh and eighth imperatives elaborate the organizational and managerial aspects of the general call to excellence of the first imperative, by addressing issues including preparing to meet risks (such as a global economic downturn), improving already strong financial management by continuing to build reserves by taking 5–10 percent annually from revenues and moving to GAAP by 2008, and enlarging the Forum's physical spaces better to accommodate conference needs of members and partners. To the non-business reader, these lists of objectives and imperatives may appear repetitive, grandiose and even impractical. But what is important to understand is that they are written within the culture and discourse of management, in which envisioning objectives and strategies of achieving them discursively is a necessary part of the process that leads to organizational change. This type of discourse is revealing, because if the organization is even reasonably effective the texts do give a plausible indication of where the organization is going.

The third text looks outward rather than inward, addressing the changing global environment in response to which the Forum needs to grow. The ten challenges for the world, as Professor Schwab described them in his address in Delhi, articulate a perspective of the interdependence of the globe and the inseparability of the economic, the political and the social in formulating approaches to meet the challenges.[4] The challenges did not appear to be ranked in a particular hierarchy. If anything, the impact each has on the other argues for the futility of attempting to rank them. Whilst most of the challenges in themselves were not unfamiliar to the audience, again Schwab's strength lay in his ability to weave a narrative that could generate imperatives for action. The *rise of China and India*, which Schwab mentioned first, is evident from the sheer weight of the size of the two economies, with China projected to be the world's largest economy by 2040 and India number three. With the two peoples comprising 35 percent of the global population, the global centre of gravity is shifting east in many ways, including consumer patterns and styles. The second challenge is *competition for global resources*, which is resulting in the repricing of commodities globally as China becomes the biggest consumer of every commodity except oil, a position that the United States retains at least for the moment. The third challenge is *management of global interdependence in a multipolar world*, which is about how to maintain stability in a world populated by many different categories of nation-state ranging from superpowers (the United States, possibly Europe, and in future China) to politically or economically unviable failed states (which according to Schwab number nearly 50 of 192 states), as well as global firms and other non-state actors. This type of management requires global scenario forecasting, as scenarios are key to framing management choices and understanding the possible consequences of those choices. Schwab envisions four global scenarios: a new world war, which could involve radical Islamists; systemic chaos, in which the current mechanisms of global governance cannot address the challenges they face successfully; continued US hegemony, as at present, but which may not be sustainable over the longer term; and a preferred scenario Schwab called "Davos World," in which the main actors would work together and undertake collective efforts to address global issues.

Schwab's fourth and fifth challenges are economic problems with huge social consequences. The *global jobs deficit* and resulting search for what Schwab calls decent work, sees a need for 40 million new jobs per year as economies grow without creating jobs, leaving 1.4 billion people beneath the poverty line worldwide. Schwab sees self-created jobs through entrepreneurship as the only way out of the dilemma, which means encouraging social as well as purely economic entrepreneurship. *Global economic imbalances in production, consumption, savings and investment patterns* require proactive policies if adjustment by economic shock is to be avoided. The $350 billion required each year to fund the US budget deficit, Schwab argues, will one day become unsustainable. Social and political responses to economic instability lead to the sixth challenge, the *search for identity in a fast changing world*. Schwab calls this the fight against negativism, extremism, fundamentalism, nationalism and protectionism. Schwab argues that Europe's pessimism about the future is a reaction to rapid globalization, and sees a global drift back from globalism toward nationalism.

The seventh challenge, *implementing the democratic challenge – the individual and the collective*, addresses the current backlash against the trend in the 1980s and 1990s toward more freedoms and more democracy. Pointing to a recent poll in Latin America showing that people would accept mild dictatorship if it would bring more economic growth, Schwab argues that people perceive the fight as being between democracy and efficiency. Democracy is threatened by the erosion of middle classes, who are the pillar of democratic systems. The eighth, and related, challenge, is *mastering intergenerational tensions – pensions, climate change, clean water, education and debt*. Addressing these key economic, social and environmental problems today is essential if successive generations are not to inherit a world dramatically worse off than conditions at present. By 2020, for example, Schwab pointed out, 50 percent of the globe's population will be living in water-stressed areas. The ninth challenge is the *fight against the unacceptable – illicit global networks, failed states, poverty, infectious diseases and lack of basic healthcare*. Poverty is unacceptable, Schwab argues, and significant pockets of the global population are not integrated into the global system or provided with basic global standards of quality of life. Failed states, terrorism, organized crime and other illicit networks are inescapably linked to the problem of poverty and the alienation it generates. The final global challenge, the *global leadership deficit*, in a sense lies behind many of the other challenges, because if it could be surmounted it would facilitate addressing all of the others. More, better global leadership is needed to manage complexity and understand new paradigms. We are unprepared even institutionally to manage a global health crisis, Schwab contended. For example, China and India should be full members of the UN Security Council and the G8. Leaders must be prepared to think in terms with new paradigms, such as the eastward shift in the global security structure, the changing roles of social institutions like family and government, a world of significantly greater transparency, and a world increasingly divided into young societies and old societies. Strong leadership must be defined by creativity in its ability to respond to challenges and turn them into opportunities.

Deftly turning the ten challenges into a call for action, Schwab outlined a three-pronged strategy for global society to meet the challenges. First, we must have a mission and the will to win the race, which requires using our human ingenuity by being creative. Second, we have to act as a global community and share fundamental beliefs. We must develop a global identity that allows us to identify and agree upon the issues that need to be solved. This global identity must be a blended identity, in the sense that we must act simultaneously as global citizens and as national citizens. This can be harder than it might appear, Schwab observed, because politicians are not elected globally. For example, we are not solving problems of the international trading system because we are not looking at solutions that are in the global long-term interest. The current political process produces compromises between national interests, but these may not serve the global long-term interest well at all. The third prong of the strategy is that we must be prepared to solve problems in what he called the "Davos spirit" using the "three Bs" approach referred to above: Binding, or problem identification; Bonding, or objective identification; and Building, or action identification. The task Schwab had set himself in the Delhi speech was ambitious. As a leader he needed to set the bar high, but he also needed to motivate the audience to act by making them feel as if real progress was indeed possible, with the Forum acting as the indispensable partner and venue for cooperation. Schwab approached his task with the combination of seriousness and effortless grace that has distinguished his public presentations throughout his career. For Schwab, the Forum clearly had its assignment cut out for it, so it was time to get busy.

Growing global leadership, preparing for the succession

Like other successful businesses, the World Economic Forum spends time thinking about and planning its own future, even as it carries out its substantive mission of thinking about the future of the world. Although he had no immediate plans to retire at the time of writing, the World Economic Forum after Klaus Schwab is very much on Professor Schwab's mind and of the mind of the Forum's senior management and Foundation Board. At age sixty-seven in 2005, perhaps Schwab's most overarching strategic objective is to ensure that the organization he created and has sustained for thirty-five years survives his retirement and continues to flourish. The core challenge for the Forum is that in order to do so, its approach to leadership will need to change fundamentally from the leader-driven organization that it has been into a collegial management model in which the organization's value and culture both define the qualifications of the leadership team and serve as the points that unify their interests. For Schwab, selecting who leads the Forum in the future is less critical than shaping the values culture that will sustain the leadership.[5]

Institutionally, this transformational process has been underway for some time. The Forum has experimented with different structures of internal management, with varying degrees of success over the years. Chains of command and accountability were more informal when the organization was smaller and was engaged in fewer areas of activity. The atmosphere was collegial and communication easy. For the first three decades of operation the Forum had a single Managing Director who reported directly to Klaus Schwab, who served as Chairman and CEO. But looking to the future, Schwab pressed for the Foundation Board to take the decision to follow the British corporate governance model in splitting clearly the supervisory functions of the Foundation Board from managerial responsibilities over the Forum. In summer 2000 the Foundation Board adopted this split of functions, with Professor Schwab assuming the role of Executive Chairman. At that time the Board also took the decision to move from having a single Managing Director to the current arrangement of having a Managing Board of five Managing Directors. Since 2000, Schwab's Executive Chairman function has included serving as Chairman of the Foundation Board and, more recently, chairing the Managing Board as well. To fulfil its objective of dividing the Forum's supervisory and managerial roles, the Foundation Board in 2005 began a search for a new Foundation Board Chairman to succeed Klaus Schwab. Professor Schwab agreed to continue to chair the Managing Board as long as he remains as fit as he was at the time of writing. Commenting on the robust level of his fitness, Schwab reported that he continues to climb at least one 4000 metre peak annually and participates in ski marathons.

Looking beyond the immediate need for institutional transformation, however, Schwab proposed a more ambitious longer-term strategy for the Forum to ensure that in future it will have both the institutional values and culture and the cadre of leaders who will embody and enact them. Schwab proposed a mechanism through which the Forum could generate its next generation of leaders internally: a stepped up, high-powered, three-year training programme run by the Forum, leading to a university master's degree. The programme, the Global Leadership Fellows Programme, which began in September 2005 under the leadership of the newest Forum Managing Director and its first Dean, Michael Obermayer, is based at the Forum's headquarters near Geneva and is being run in conjunction with two of the top graduate schools in North America and Europe, the Kennedy School of Government at Harvard and the London Business School. The degree conferred will be a master's degree in global leadership from the newly constituted, Swiss-licensed World Economic Forum University. In this respect, the Forum joins the World Trade Organization in constituting itself as an educational body for a specific purpose, as the WTO is already running a degree-awarding training and study programme focusing on international trade. That notwithstanding, the Forum once again is creating a unique and hybrid model, in this case for training and education. The trainees, who pay no tuition fees and are paid a stipend, pursue their studies through a series of work assignments at the Forum and at partner firms, interspersed with academic study modules that generally are run intensively according to the "executive education" model. Coursework will be broadly divided into two categories: knowledge, focusing on understanding the world and action in it, through courses on topics such as strategy development and implementation, international relations and political economy; and personal and interpersonal skills, through courses such as project management and group leadership, public speaking, and coaching and mentoring. In addition, students will work closely with mentors on the Forum's staff to learn about the institution and for assistance in developing their own study programme.[6] The Forum's objective is to be able to select its future senior management cadre from amongst the graduates, who will not only have obtained set of qualifications and skills that the Forum staff regard as essential to thinking about and undertaking leadership of global issues and of organizations such as the Forum, but will also in the process have been socialized into the values culture, norms and modes of operation of the Forum itself.

The initial response to the announcement of the Global Leadership Fellows Programme was very favourable. By the 15 May 2005 application deadline for the initial class, the Forum had received 1800 applications. Over 600 of the applicants had MBAs or JDs from top business and law schools. The Forum accepted forty-six students into the pioneer GLF class and is targeting an intake of thirty for the September 2006 cohort. If the new programme can be understood as in effect a multi-stage apprenticeship for senior management at the Forum, their clear success in attracting high-quality applicants holds significant promise in terms of then allowing Forum senior management to make further hiring selections for future Forum jobs from amongst those graduates who perform best in the programme itself. As graduates take up senior management posts at member and partner firms of the Forum, it will also constitute a new level of interrelationship between the firms and the Forum, and between the firms themselves, which may facilitate the ability of the firms to function as a network in cooperating on the major global, regional and industry agenda items pursued by the Forum, as well as facilitating cooperation at a purely business level.

Conclusions

As the old saying goes, "imitation is the sincerest form of flattery." One indicator of the Forum's success at creating a new institutional structure for global problem solving and governance is the increasing numbers of imitators, if not yet in a plausible sense competitors. Organizations such as Forbes Magazine are sponsoring business leadership conferences with titles such as "The Forbes CEO Forum," to which a range of stakeholders are invited to participate. The 2005 Forbes CEO Forum featured former US President George Bush the Elder, among other notables.[7] Not only by appropriating terms like Forum is the emulation of the style and approach apparent at such gatherings. Former US President Bill Clinton, himself one of the biggest supporters of the World Economic Forum, organized a very successful high-level gathering in September 2005 in New York called the "Clinton Global Initiative." Speakers included UK Prime Minister Tony Blair, Nigerian President Olusegun Obasanjo, Jordan's King Abdullah, News Corp. CEO Rupert Murdoch, and General Electric CEO Jeff Immelt. Clinton said the gathering was patterned on the Forum's Davos Annual Meeting, but Clinton expected of his attendees that they would be prepared to make specific commitments to act on the conference themes of fighting poverty, easing religious conflict and reducing environmental degradation.[8] The Forum's strategy documents indicate that they recognize these undertakings both as compliments to the success of the approach that the Forum has developed and as challenges to be met in terms of the need to continue to develop and improve in order to stay the best and to continue to be perceived as the best of breed. The deeper implication of the emulation trend suggests that a broader mode of global governance may be emerging in which organizations such as the World Economic Forum will play a pivotal role as catalysts bringing together global, regional and local stakeholders of different types to shape agendas and solve problems. The Forum itself increasingly highlights its agenda-shaping role and aspirations in this regard. Whether this mode of governance proves to be a new type of global democracy in the sense that it is laterally networked and driven by popular perceptions of legitimacy, or whether it ultimately is perceived as a series of elite-driven networks of the already rich and powerful acting in their own interests, will in large part hinge on the ability of organizations like the World Economic Forum to live up to their own stated principles and objectives and, equally critically, upon their ability to communicate effectively to the global public through public diplomacy.

The introduction to this book articulated two narratives of the World Economic Forum's evolution: the Forum as Shar-pei, born with baggy skin only to grow into a sleek creature of neoliberal globalization, and the Wolf in Sheep's Clothing, a rangy beast for promoting private deals for private gain whilst clothed in the respectability of global service. In light of the preceding investigation, two observations arise. One, as narratives the "Shar-pei" and the "Wolf in Sheep's Clothing" may not be as far apart as they initially appear; and two, as narratives of the Forum's evolution both may be more than a bit off the mark. Cuddly though it may be, the Shar-pei can bite, as many creatures of the neoliberal global economy have been shown to do. Equally though, the wolf, whether it be in sheep's clothing or not, is a necessary part of the global ecosystem, and where wolves were hunted to extinction they have had to be replaced through breeding programs in order to restore balance to regional ecologies. Global capitalism by its nature has a competitive, even predatory element, but that need not negate the shared exercise of social responsibilities for global governance. Through its own ever improving efforts to tell its story to the global public, the Forum over the past fifteen years has effectively stripped off whatever sheep's clothing it might have been seen to wear previously, leaving the wolf and the Shar-pei as different but not-so-very-different denizens of the narrative landscape of global political economy. At the turn of the twenty-first century, when fresh battle lines were drawn between proponents of neoliberal globalization and those who challenged it, arguing that "another world is possible," it was easy enough for each side to embrace the narrative of the Forum's evolution that sited the organization on one side or the other in the contest of how the global economy was to grow. But by 2006 those who still embrace either narrative might be seen to be clinging to images that are at best historical and at worst simply dated. The dot.crash, the protests at Seattle and Genoa, the Kleptogate scandals, the attacks of 11 September 2001, all have demonstrated to the global public that the idea of a neoliberal version of globalization as triumphant and inevitable, which perhaps reached its zenith in the 1990s, is essentially contested from many directions. Crucially, the multi-stakeholder model of global governance supported by the World Economic Forum is one of the central forces challenging the notion of markets and firms ruling untrammeled over other social forces and interests. The Forum's staff argue that "entrepreneurship in the global public interest" has always been at the core of the Forum's mission. Whether they succeeded in convincing many of their critics prior to the 2000s is another question. But just as many, if by no means all, erstwhile critics of the Forum have realized that an effective way to articulate their agenda and objectives is to do so within the Forum itself, many individuals and firms who have sought to profit from increasingly global markets have realized that taking account of other types of stakeholders in the venues that the Forum has created is necessary to create the value that they seek. In this set of disparate realizations lies a narrative that is still being written of a new, emerging, and in an important sense democratic, form of global governance, the consequences and implications of which may not yet be able to be foreseen by conventional theoretical and empirical understandings of global political economy and diplomacy today.

Notes

Introduction

1 The two narratives were described in greater detail in Geoffrey Allen Pigman, "A Multifunctional Case Study for Teaching International Political Economy: The World Economic Forum as Shar-pei or Wolf in Sheep's Clothing?," *International Studies Perspectives* 3 (August 2002): 291–309.

2 This public policy dilemma is discussed theoretically in Bossert's critique of the Kaldor compensation test, which addresses the problem of making welfare economic recommendations based on utility possibilities sets associated with various sets of feasible alternatives. See Walter Bossert, "The Kaldor Compensation Test and Rational Choice," *Journal of Public Economics* 59 (1996): 265–76.

3 The implication of Bossert's argument against the Kaldor compensation test is that, in the absence of a guarantee that compensation or sidepayments would be made to make liberalization Pareto-optimal, it would be unjustified for a government to prefer liberalization policies over non-liberalizing policies. See Bossert, *ibid.*: 266. Hence finding a political mechanism to ensure that sidepayments are made becomes a much more important nation-state public policy objective for supporters of market-liberalizing globalization.

1 A multi-stakeholder approach

1 Jean-Jacques Servan-Schreiber, *The American Challenge* (New York: Atheneum, 1968); David P. Calleo and Benjamin M. Rowland, *America and the World Political Economy* (Bloomington IN: Indiana University Press, 1973): 92–3; Henry R. Nau, *The Myth of America's Decline* (Oxford: Oxford University Press, 1990): 140–57.

2 Calleo and Rowland, *ibid.*: 162–91.

3 Robert W. Cox, "Globalization, Multilateralism, and Democracy," in Robert W. Cox with Timothy J. Sinclair, *Approaches to World Order* (Cambridge: Cambridge University Press, 1996): 524–36.

4 A good substantive discussion highlighting the differences between phenomena of globalization and the globalization discourse can be found in Colin Hay, "Contemporary Capitalism, Globalization, Regionalization

and the Persistence of National Variation," *Review of International Studies* 26, 4, (2000): 509–31. Linda Weiss gives a useful account of the academic debate between globalists and skeptics as she critiques the often-assumed antinomy between the global and the national principles of organization. *See* Linda Weiss "Globalization and national governance: antinomy or interdependence?," *Review of International Studies* 25, special issue (December 1999): 59–88.

5 Interview with Klaus Schwab, Cologny, Switzerland, May 2005; Joyce Wadler, "The 'Chief Visionary' Discusses His Creation," *New York Times* (31 January 2002), at http://www.nytimes.com, accessed 31 January 2002.

6 Joyce Wadler, *ibid.*

7 Kirsten Lundberg, "Convener or Player? The World Economic Forum and Davos," *Kennedy School of Government Case programme* C15-04-1741.0 (Cambridge MA: Harvard University, 2004): 4.

8 Lundberg, *ibid.*: 5.

9 "Modern Business Management in the Machining Industry" (tr. Anthony Deos).

10 Interview with Klaus Schwab, Cologny, Switzerland, May 2005.

11 Interview with Klaus Schwab, Cologny, Switzerland, May 2005.

12 World Economic Forum, *About the Forum, History*, at http://www.worldeconomicforum.org, accessed 2000; Lundberg, "Convener or Player? The World Economic Forum and Davos," 6.

13 Lundberg, "Convener or Player? The World Economic Forum and Davos," 12.

14 World Economic Forum, *About the Forum, History, 1970–79*, at http://www.worldeconomicforum.org, accessed 12 January 2000.

15 Lundberg, "Convener or Player? The World Economic Forum and Davos," 11.

16 World Economic Forum (2000) *Members and Constituents, Foundation Members*, at http://www.worldeconomicforum.org, accessed 2000.

17 Lundberg, "Convener or Player? The World Economic Forum and Davos," 9.

18 *Ibid.*: 7–9.

19 *Ibid.*

20 "A Steady Climb to Success," *Business Standard (New Delhi)* (26/27 November 2005, India Economic Summit 2005 special section): 2.

21 *Financial Times* World Economic Forum Guide, "Timeline: Thirty Years of Schmooze," at http://www.ft.com/specials/sp51b2.htm, accessed 11 September 2000.

22 Lundberg, "Convener or Player? The World Economic Forum and Davos," 24.

23 World Economic Forum, *History and Achievements*, at http://www.weforum.org, accessed 25 October 2004.

24 Lundberg, "Convener or Player? The World Economic Forum and Davos," 26–7.

25 World Economic Forum (2000) *About the Forum, History*, at http://www.worldeconomicforum.org, accessed 2000.

26 Lundberg, "Convener or Player? The World Economic Forum and Davos," 26–7.

27 Charles Overbeek, "Davos 98; The World Economic Forum Strikes Again," at http://www.parascope.com (2000), accessed 2000; *Financial*

Times World Economic Forum Guide, "Timeline: Thirty Years of Schmooze," at http://www.ft.com/specials/sp51b2.htm, accessed 11 September 2000.

28 Lundberg, "Convener or Player? The World Economic Forum and Davos," 27.

29 *Ibid.*: 24–25.

30 World Economic Forum (2000), *About the Forum, History*, at http://www.worldeconomicforum.org, accessed 2000.

31 In the 2000 US presidential election, Gore won the national popular vote by over 500,000 votes over that of his closest competitor. Bill Clinton's presidential successor, George W. Bush, sent a representative to the 2000 Davos Summit, New Jersey Governor Christine Todd Whitman, whom Bush subsequently appointed to head the Environmental Protection Agency.

32 Breffini O'Rourke, "World: Davos's Smooth Surface Ruffled By Controversy," Radio Free Europe/Radio Liberty, at http://www.rferl.org (27 January 2000), accessed 2000.

33 Will Hutton, "Quixote's Horse: For Davos Man, Greed Is Good, Too Good to Be True," *Guardian* (30 January 2000).

34 Guy de Jonquières and Holly Yeager, "Davos Goes West," *Financial Times* (25 January 2002).

35 *Ibid.*

36 Leslie Eaton, "For City, Good Buzz May Be Best Payoff of Economic Forum," *New York Times* (30 January 2002), at http://www.nytimes.com, accessed 30 January 2002.

37 Cristyne Nicholas, quoted in *ibid.*

38 Confidential security memorandum from global financial services firm to New York staff, emailed 29 January 2002.

39 Alex Kuczynski, "Parties Planned for World Economic Forum," *New York Times* (27 January 2002), at http://www.nytimes.com, accessed 31 January 2002.

40 Charles McLean, quoted in Guy de Jonquières and Holly Yeager, "Davos Goes West," *Financial Times* (25 January 2002).

2 Purposes public and private

1 Kirsten Lundberg, "Convener or Player? The World Economic Forum and Davos," *Kennedy School of Government Case programme* C15-04-1741.0 (Cambridge MA: Harvard University, 2004): 13.

2 Interview with Peter Torreele, World Economic Forum Managing Director, Cologny, Switzerland, May 2005.

3 World Economic Forum *Annual Report 2004/2005*.

4 Background interview material provided by World Economic Forum staff, October 2005.

5 Interviews with Peter Torreele and Richard Samans, World Economic Forum Managing Directors, Cologny, Switzerland, May 2005.

6 June 2005.

7 Interview with Peter Torreele, Cologny, Switzerland, May 2005.

8 Interview with Gary Shainberg, Vice President for Technology and Innovation, BT Group, New Delhi, India, November 2005.

9 Interview with senior manager, Deloitte, Touche Tomatsu, November 2005.

10 Interview with senior manager, World Economic Forum Strategic Partner firm, April 2005.
11 In April 2006 one Swiss franc was worth approximately 0.63, £0.44 and US$0.77.
12 World Economic Forum 2006, *About Us, Technology Pioneers*, http://www.weforum.org, accessed 10 January 2006.
13 World Economic Forum 2006, *About Us, Young Global Leaders*, www.weforum.org, accessed 10 January 2006.
14 World Economic Forum 2006, *About Us, Women Leaders Programme*, http://www.weforum.org, accessed 16 January 2006.
15 World Economic Forum 2003, "Guidelines how the World Economic Forum fosters and supports communities," internal strategy document, 23 April.
16 Synergos Institute 2006, http://www.synergos.org, accessed 16 January 2006.
17 World Economic Forum 2006, *About Us, Communities*, http://www.weforum.org, accessed 16 January 2006; Schwab Foundation for Social Entrepreneurship 2006, http://www.schwabfound.org, accessed 16 January 2006.
18 World Economic Forum 2004, *Foundation Board*, http://www.weforum.org, accessed 25 October 2004.
19 Lundberg, "Convener or Player? The World Economic Forum and Davos:" 18.
20 Interview with Klaus Schwab, Cologny, Switzerland, May 2005.
21 Lundberg, "Convener or Player? The World Economic Forum and Davos," 15–16.
22 Interview with Ged Davis, World Economic Forum Managing Director, Cologny, Switzerland, May 2005.
23 Since 2000 the Forum has continued to test different organizational structures for its activities, adjusting and renaming the Centres as its strategic plan evolves.
24 World Economic Forum 2006, *About Us, Leadership Team*, http://www.weforum.org, accessed 10 January 2006.
25 World Economic Forum 2006, *About Us, Leadership Team*, http://www.weforum.org, accessed 10 January 2006; Troika Dialog Troika.ru 2006, *About, Board of Directors*, http://www.troika.ru, accessed 10 January 2006; Intrepid Learning Solutions 2006, *About Intrepid, Advisory Board*, http://www.intrepidls.com, accessed 10 January 2006.
26 World Economic Forum 2006, *About Us, Leadership Team*, http://www.weforum.org, accessed 10 January 2006. Management team numbers are as reflected on the Forum website in January 2006.
27 World Economic Forum (2005) *Annual Report 2004/2005*.
28 Lundberg, "Convener or Player? The World Economic Forum and Davos," 14.
29 *Ibid.*: 27.
30 Charles Overbeek, "Davos 98; The World Economic Forum Strikes Again," *Parascope* (2000), http://www.parascope.com, accessed 2001.
31 *Ibid.*
32 PriceWaterhouseCoopers 1999, *Inside the Mind of the CEO; Retrospective from James J. Schiro*, http://www.pwcglobal.com/gx/eng/ins-sol/spec-int/davos/about.html, accessed 28 December 2000.

33 Interview with Peter Torreele, Cologny, Switzerland, May 2005.
34 For discussions of the notion of *Lebenswelt* and its impact upon communicative action and diplomacy, *vide* Jürgen Habermas, *On the Pragmatics of Social Interaction* (Cambridge MA: MIT Press, 2001): vii–xiv, 44–64; Harald Mueller, "International Relations as Communicative Action," 160–78, in Karin M. Fierke and Knud Erik Jörgensen, *Constructing International Relations: The Next Generation* (Armonk NY: M. E. Sharpe, 2001); Lars G. Löse, "Communicative Action and the World of Diplomacy," 179–200, in Fierke and Jörgensen, *Constructing International Relations: The Next Generation.*

3 The Forum in contemporary global society

1 Friedrich V. Kratochwil, "Constructivism as an Approach to Interdisciplinary Study," in Karin M. Fierke and Knud Erik Jørgensen, *Constructing International Relations; the next generation* (Armonk NY: M. E. Sharpe, 2001), 13–35; Alexander Wendt, "Ideas all the Way Down?," in *Social Construction of International Politics* (Cambridge: Cambridge University Press, 1999), ch. 3.
2 Adam Watson, *Diplomacy: The Dialogue Between States* (London: Routledge, 1984); G. R. Berridge, *Diplomacy: Theory and Practice*, 3rd edn (London: Palgrave, 2005).
3 Donna Lee and David Hudson, "The Old and New Significance of Political Economy in Diplomacy," *Review of International Studies* 30 (2004), June; Kishan S. Rana, *Inside Diplomacy*, revised paperback edn (New Delhi: Manas Publications, 2002).
4 G. A. Pigman, "Making Room at the Negotiating Table: The Growth of Diplomacy Between Nation-state Governments and Non-state Economic Entities," *Diplomacy and Statecraft* 16, 2 (June 2005): 385–401.
5 Interview with Richard Samans, World Economic Forum Managing Director, Cologny, Switzerland, May 2005.
6 Interview with Ged Davis, World Economic Forum Managing Director, Cologny, Switzerland, May 2005.
7 European Management Forum publication 1976, cited in Kirsten Lundberg, "Convener or Player? The World Economic Forum and Davos," *Kennedy School of Government Case programme* C15-04-1741.0 (Cambridge MA: Harvard University, 2004): 39.
8 European Management Forum promotional document "The EMF," 1983, cited in Lundberg, *ibid.*
9 World Economic Forum, *Report from the President 1993*, cited in Lundberg, *ibid.*
10 World Economic Forum, "The World Economic Forum: Entrepreneurship in the Global Public Interest," promotional brochure (2005).
11 Forumblog.org – the World Economic Forum weblog, at http://www.wef.typepad.com/blog, accessed 27 July 2005.
12 World Economic Forum (2004) *About Us*, at http://www.weforum.com, accessed 25 October 2004.
13 World Economic Forum, "The World Economic Forum: Entrepreneurship in the Global Public Interest," promotional brochure (2005).

4 Generating knowledge today

1 World Economic Forum, "Global Town Hall Report," 26 January 2005, http://www.weforum.org/site/homepublic.nsf/Content/Annual+Meeting+ 2005, accessed 18 February 2005.

2 Samuel P. Huntington, Keynote Address, Colorado College 125th Anniversary Symposium, "Cultures in the 21st Century: Conflicts and Convergences," 4 February 1999, http://www.coloradocollege.edu/academics/ anniversary/Transcripts/HuntingtonTXT.htm, accessed 20 February 2005; Timothy Garton Ash, "Davos Man's Death Wish," *Guardian* (3 February 2005), http://www.guardian.co.uk, accessed 20 February 2005.

3 Timothy L. O'Brien, "Can Angelina Jolie Really Save the World?" *New York Times* (30 January 2005), http://www.nytimes.com, accessed 1 February 2005; World Economic Forum (2005) "Participants 'Get Down to Business' On First Day of World Economic Forum Annual Meeting 2005 in Davos," http://www.weforum.org, accessed 28 January 2005.

4 World Economic Forum, "Global Town Hall Report," 26 January 2005, http://www.weforum.org/site/homepublic.nsf/Content/Annual+Meeting+ 2005, accessed 18 February 2005.

5 "2003 Most Powerful Women in International Business," *Fortune*, 13 October 2003, http://www.fortune.com/fortune/powerwomen/2003/global/ snapshot/0,18687,40,00.html, accessed 29 April 2004.

6 Lubna Olayan, "A Saudi Vision For Growth," keynote address to Jeddah Economic Forum, 17 January 2004, Saudi-US Relations Information Service, http://www.saudi-us-relations.org/newsletter2004/saudi-relations-interest-01-21.html, accessed 29 April 2005.

7 World Economic Forum "Special Address by Tony Blair, Prime Minister of the United Kingdom," 27 January 2005, http://www.weforum.org, accessed 28 January 2005.

8 Krishna Guha, "Doubts Over US Social Security Reform," *Financial Times*, 29 January 2005, http://www.ft.com, accessed 31 January 2005.

9 Krishna Guha, "Pakistan to Offer India Kashmir-free Project Deals," *Financial Times*, 30 January 2005, http://www.ft.com; Tim Weber, "Pakistan Pushes India on Pipeline," BBC News, http://www.bbc.co.uk, 31 January 2005, accessed 31 January 2005.

10 Tim Weber, "Pakistan Pushes India on Pipeline," BBC News, http://www.bbc.co.uk, 31 January 2005, accessed 31 January 2005.

11 Michael McKee, "Soros Says Kerry's Failings Undermined Campaign Against Bush," *Bloomberg.com*, 30 January 2005, http://www.bloomberg. com, accessed 31 January 2005.

12 James Hertling and Simon Clark, "Bill Gates, World's Richest Man, Bets Against Dollar (Update 3)," *Bloomberg.com*, 29 January 2005; James Hertling, "Chinese Officials Back 'Stable' Currency, Rebuff Global Appeal," *Bloomberg.com*, 29 January, http://www.bloomberg.com, accessed 31 January 2005.

13 Alan Beattie and Krishna Guha, "Chirac's Tax Plans to Fund Aid Fail to Convince," *Financial Times*, 27 January 2005, http://www.ft.com, accessed 28 January 2005.

14 Krishna Guha, "BP Chief Slams Rise of 'Pseudo Markets,' " *Financial Times*, 27 January 2005, http://www.ft.com, accessed 28 January 2005.

15 Tim Weber, "WTO Boss Pushes for Trade Deal," BBC News, 28 January 2005, http://www.bbc.co.uk, accessed 28 January 2005.
16 Klaus Schwab cited in video "The Spirit of Davos," http://www.weforum.org /site/homepublic.nsf/Content/Annual+Meeting+2005, viewed 18 February 2005.
17 Jose Maria Figueres cited in "The Spirit of Davos," *ibid.*
18 Michael Foale cited in *ibid.*
19 The video entitled "The Spirit of Davos" as it appeared in early 2005 was no longer available for viewing on the Forum website, having been replaced with a different, ten-minute video bearing the same name containing a montage of scenes of the 2005 Davos Annual Meeting.
20 David Smith and William Lewis, "Corporate Big Shots Swagger at Davos," *Sunday Times* (London) 30 January 2005: 10.
21 Howard Webster, "Never Mind the Economy, Where's Sharon Stone?" *Sunday Times* (London) 30 January 2005, News Review: 9.
22 Tim Weber, "Davos Touches the MTV Generation," BBC News, 25 January 2005, http://www.bbc.co.uk, accessed 31 January 2005.
23 Benjamin Zander quoted in Tim Weber, "Davos Touches the MTV Generation," BBC News, 25 January 2005, http://www.bbc.co.uk, accessed 31 January 2005.
24 Klaus Schwab quoted in Timothy L. O'Brien, "Can Angelina Jolie Really Save the World?" *New York Times, op. cit.*; "Participants 'Get Down to Business' On First Day of World Economic Forum Annual Meeting 2005 in Davos," 26 January 2005, http://www.weforum.org, accessed 28 January 2005.
25 *Ibid.*
26 Timothy Garton Ash, "Davos Man's Death Wish," *Guardian*, 3 February 2005, http://www.guardian.co.uk, accessed 20 February 2005.
27 David Smith, "A Good Week in Brown's Mission to Save the World," *Sunday Times* (London) 30 January 2005, News Review: 9.
28 William Lewis, "Danger Lurks In Sec's Hedge Fund Halfway House," *Sunday Times* (London) 30 January 2005: 4.
29 Planning Commission, Government of India 2006, *About Us: History*, http://www.planningcommission.nic.in, accessed 17 January 2006.
30 World Economic Forum, "India Town Hall: Becoming a Top-Ten Competitive Economy in Ten Years," 2005 India Economic Summit session summary, 27 November 2005, http://www.weforum.org, accessed 19 January 2006.
31 World Economic Forum 2005, Prime Minister's Speech at India Economic Summit, handout, 29 November 2005.

5 Discourse, research and action

1 Colin Hay, "Contemporary Capitalism, Globalization, Regionalization and the Persistence of National Variation," *Review of International Studies* 26, 4 (2000): 509–31.
2 Robert W. Cox, *Production, Power, and World Order* (New York: Columbia University Press, 1987), 211–30.
3 On discourse theory *vide* Michel Foucault, *The History of Sexuality* (London: Penguin Books, 1976); Jean-François Lyotard, *The Postmodern*

Condition: A Report on Knowledge (Manchester: Manchester University Press, 1984); Jens Bartelson, *A Genealogy of Sovereignty* (Cambridge: Cambridge University Press, 1995). On discourse analysis *vide* Peter Preston, *Discourses of Development* (Aldershot: Avebury, 1994); Geoffrey Allen Pigman, "The Sovereignty Discourse and the US Debate on Joining the World Trade Organization," *Global Society* 12, 1 (1998): 75–102.

4 World Economic Forum 2001, Annual Meeting, *A Brief History of the Annual Meeting*, http://www.worldeconomicforum.org, accessed 2001.

5 World Economic Forum, *What We Do, Davos Annual Meeting 2001*, http://www.weforum.org, accessed 2001.

6 World Economic Forum 2001, Davos Summit panel, *The Corporation and the Public*, 27 January 2001, http://www.weforum.org, accessed 2001.

7 Ronald J. Deibert, "International Plug 'n' Play? Citizen Activism, the Internet, and Global Public Policy," *International Studies Perspectives* 1 (2000): 255–72.

8 *Ibid.*

9 Robert O'Brien, Anne Marie Goetz, Jan Aart Scholte and Mark Williams, *Contesting Global Governance: Multilateral Economic Institutions and Global Social Movements* (Cambridge: Cambridge University Press 2000), 206–34.

10 Nik Gowing, interview with Charles McLean, BBC World Television, 25 January 2001.

11 Kirsten Lundberg, "Convener or Player? The World Economic Forum and Davos," *Kennedy School of Government Case programme* C15-04-1741.0 (Cambridge MA: Harvard University Press, 2004), 19–20.

12 Prices consulted were from Amazon.com, http://www.amazon.com, accessed 22 January 2006.

13 Jeffrey Sachs and Andrew M. Warner, "Why Competitiveness Counts," in World Economic Forum, *Global Competitiveness Report* (Oxford: Oxford University Press, 1996), 8–13.

14 Lundberg, "Convener or Player? The World Economic Forum and Davos," 19–20.

15 Xavier Sala-i-Martin, "Executive Summary," World Economic Forum, *Global Competitiveness Report 2003–2004* (Oxford: Oxford University Press, 2004), xi.

16 Lundberg, "Convener or Player? The World Economic Forum and Davos," 19–20.

17 *Ibid.*

18 Xavier Sala-i-Martin, "Executive Summary," *Global Competitiveness Report 2003–2004* (Oxford: Oxford University Press, 2004), xi.

19 World Economic Forum, *Global Competitiveness Report 2004–2005* (London: Palgrave Macmillan, 2005), xiii.

20 Michael Porter, "Building the Microeconomic Foundations of Prosperity," in World Economic Forum, *Global Competitiveness Report 2003–2004* (Oxford: Oxford University Press, 2004), 31.

21 Xavier Sala-i-Martin, "Executive Summary," in World Economic Forum, *Global Competitiveness Report 2003–2004* (Oxford: Oxford University Press, 2004), xi.

22 Emma Loades and Maria Angeles-Oliva, "Measuring Competitiveness with the Executive Opinion Survey," in World Economic Forum, *Global*

Competitiveness Report 2003–2004 (Oxford: Oxford University Press, 2004), 167–78.

23 Jeffrey Sachs and Andrew M. Warner, "Why Competitiveness Counts," in World Economic Forum, *Global Competitiveness Report* (Oxford: Oxford University Press, 1996), 8–13.

24 Jeffrey Sachs and Andrew M. Warner, "The Social Welfare State and Competitiveness," in World Economic Forum, *Global Competitiveness Report* (Oxford: Oxford University Press, 1996), 20–6.

25 Frederick Hu and Jeffrey Sachs (1996) "Executive Summary," in World Economic Forum, *Global Competitiveness Report* (Oxford: Oxford University Press, 1996), 14–19.

26 Claude Smajda, "Beyond the Statistics," in World Economic Forum, *Global Competitiveness Report* (Oxford: Oxford University Press, 1996), 28–31.

27 Daniel Kaufmann, "Governance Redux: The Empirical Challenge," World Economic Forum *Global Competitiveness Report 2003–2004* (Oxford: Oxford University Press 2004), 137.

28 *Ibid.*: 142.

29 *Ibid.*

30 *Ibid.*: 145.

31 Klaus Schwab, "Preface," in World Economic Forum, *Global Competitiveness Report 2001–2002* (New York/Oxford: Oxford University Press, 2002), 10.

32 *Ibid.*: 12.

33 *Ibid.*: 12–13.

34 Fiona Paua, "Global Diffusion of ICT: A Progress Report," World Economic Forum, *Global Information Technology Report 2003–2004: Towards an Equitable Information Society* (Oxford: Oxford University Press, 2004), 23–56.

35 infoDev, the Information for Development programme 2006, *About Us*, http://www.infodev.org, accessed 22 January 2006.

36 Klaus Schwab "Preface," in World Economic Forum, *Global Information Technology Report 2003–04: Towards an Equitable Information Society* (Oxford: Oxford University Press, 2004), v.

37 Jose-Maria Figueres-Olsen, "Introduction," in World Economic Forum, *Global Information Technology Report 2003–04: Towards an Equitable Information Society* (Oxford: Oxford University Press, 2004), vii.

38 *Ibid.*

39 Petri Rouvinen and Pekka Ylä-Anttila, "Case Study: Little Finland's Transformation to a Wireless Giant," in World Economic Forum, *Global Information Technology Report 2003–2004: Towards an Equitable Information Society* (Oxford: Oxford University Press, 2004), 87–108.

40 Bruno Lanvin and Christine Zhen-Wei Qiang, "Poverty 'e-Readication:' Using ICT to Meet MDG: Direct and Indirect Roles of e-Maturity," in World Economic Forum, *Global Information Technology Report 2003–2004: Towards an Equitable Information Society* (Oxford: Oxford University Press, 2004), 57–70.

41 Interview with Richard Samans, World Economic Forum Managing Director, Cologny, Switzerland, May 2005.

42 Interview with Ged Davis, World Economic Forum Managing Director, Cologny, Switzerland, May 2005.

43 World Economic Forum 2006, *Initiatives, Disaster Resource Network*, http://www.weforum.org, accessed 22 January 2006.
44 World Economic Forum 2006, *Initiatives, International Monetary Convention Project*, http://www.weforum.org, accessed 22 January 2006.
45 World Economic Forum 2003, *Agricultural Trade Task Force, Communiqué of Recommendations*, 17 June, http://www.weforum.org, accessed 2 November 2005.
46 *Ibid.*
47 "Global Economic Prospects and the Developing Countries 2002: Making Trade Work for the World's Poor," World Bank 2001, as cited in *Communiqué of Recommendations, op. cit.*
48 World Economic Forum 2003, *Agricultural Trade Task Force, Communiqué of Recommendations*.
49 *Ibid.*
50 *Ibid.*
51 McKinsey & Company, "Building Effective Public-Private Partnerships: Lessons Learnt from the Jordan Education Initiative" (2005); World Economic Forum 2004, "Jordan Education Initiative; A Public-private Partnership Model for Effective and Advanced Learning Deployment," publicity pamphlet.
52 *Ibid.*
53 *Ibid.*
54 *Ibid.*

6   Engaging the critics

1 Jean Christophe Graz, "How Powerful are Transnational Elite Clubs? The Social Myth of the World Economic Forum," *New Political Economy* 8, 3 (November 2003): 321–40.
2 Antonio Gramsci, *Selections from the Prison Notebooks*, eds and trans. Quintin Hoare and Geoffrey Smith (London: Lawrence and Wishart, 1971).
3 Robert W. Cox, "Gramsci, Hegemony, and International Relations: An Essay in Method," in Robert W. Cox with Timothy J. Sinclair, *Approaches to World Order* (Cambridge: Cambridge University Press, 1996): 124–43.
4 Ronald J. Deibert, "International Plug 'n' Play? Citizen Activism, the Internet, and Global Public Policy," *International Studies Perspectives* 1 (2000): 255–72.
5 Charles Overbeek, "Davos 98; The World Economic Forum Strikes Again," *Parascope.com* (2000) http://www.parascope.com, accessed 2001.
6 Ronald J. Deibert, "International Plug 'n' Play? Citizen Activism, the Internet, and Global Public Policy," *International Studies Perspectives* 1 (2000): 255–72.
7 Alain Kessi, "Mobilize against the World Economic Forum in Davos, Swiss Alps," leaflet (25 December 1999) translated, http://www.flag/blackened.net/global/100davos.htm, accessed 2001.
8 *Ibid.*
9 "Davos. Deux visions de la mondialisation," *Le Telegramme de Bretagne*, 30 January 2000.
10 "Jose Bové: 'Le mélange entre intérêts politiques et financiers est détestable'," *Libération*, 29/30, January 2000. Bové:

il y a deux forums. L'un est public. L'autre est non-officiel, voire secret, et il abrite tous les contacts et les discussions qui ont lieu en coulisses entre les multinationales et les chefs d'Etat et de gouvernement. Discussions qui portent non seulement sur des contrats, mais aussi sur des politiques à suivre.

[There are two forums. One is public. The other is unofficial, even secret, and it accommodates all contacts and discussions that take place behind the scenes between multinational firms and heads of state and government. Discussions that address not only deals, but also the politics that flow from them.]

11 "Jose Bové: 'Le mélange entre intérêts politiques et financiers est détestable'," *Libération*, 29/30 January 2000.

12 *Berne Declaration*, "Berne Declaration Response to Davos," press release, 2000, http://www.davosnewsbies.com, accessed 2001.

13 Common Dreams News Wire, "Davos: Groups Launch 'Citizens Compact' on the UN and Corporations," 28 December 2000, http://www.commondreams.org, accessed 2001.

14 *Berne Declaration,* "The Public Eye on Davos," 2001, http://www.Davos2001.ch/eye.htm, accessed 2001.

15 Gustavo Capdevila, "Unique Awards Highlight Corporate Irresponsibility," Inter Press Service, 29 January 2005, http://www.commondreams.org, accessed 5 October 2005.

16 Raymond Colitt, "Parallel Forum Provides Alternative," *Financial Times/www.ft.com*, 25 January 2001.

17 Steve Kingstone, "World Social Forum Gets Under Way," BBC News, 28 January 2005, http://www.bbc.com, accessed 28 January 2005; Raymond Colitt, "World Social Forum Opens in Porto Alegre," *FT.com*, 26 January 2005, http://www.ft.com, accessed 28 January 2005.

18 Steve Kingstone, "Unity and Diversity at 'other Davos'," BBC News, 31 January 2005, http://www.bbc.com, accessed 31 January 2005.

19 World Economic Forum 2006, *Events, Annual Meeting, Open Forum*, http://www.weforum.org, accessed 25 January 2006.

20 Amnesty International 2006, "World Social Forum/World Economic Forum," web.amnesty.org/pages/ec-worldfora-eng, accessed 26 January 2006.

21 Emad Mekay, "Davos and Porto Alegre Pursue Identical Aims, Says WEF Chief," *Inter Press News Service Agency*, 25 January 2003.

22 World Economic Forum 2005, Klaus Schwab statement at panel session, "Global Challenges and India," World Economic Forum India Economic Summit, 28 November 2005.

23 Interview with Managing Director and COO Andre Schneider, Cologny, Switzerland, May 2005.

24 Steve Kingstone, "World Social Forum Gets Under Way," BBC News, 28 January 2005, http://www.bbc.com, accessed 28 January 2005.

25 Larry Elliot, "CBI Chief Claims Davos Hijacked by NGOs," *Guardian*, 31 January 2005.

26 Augusto Lopez-Claros and Saadia Zahidi (2005) "Women's Empowerment: Measuring the Global Gender Gap" (Cologny/Geneva: World Economic Forum) p. 1.

27 World Economic Forum (2006) *About Us, Women Leaders Programme*, http://www.weforum.org, accessed 2006; Lopez-Claros, Augusto and Saadia Zahidi, "Women's Empowerment: Measuring the Global Gender Gap" (Cologny/Geneva: World Economic Forum, 2005).

28 Breffini O'Rourke, "World: Davos's Smooth Surface Ruffled By Controversy," Radio Free Europe/Radio Liberty, http://www.rferl.org, 27 January 2000.

29 Joyce Wadler, "The 'Chief Visionary' Discusses His Creation," *New York Times*, 31 January 2002, http://www.nytimes.com, accessed 31 January 2002.

30 Tony Perkins, "Davos dispatch," *Redherring*, http://www.redherring.com, 29 January 2000.

31 Joyce Wadler, "The 'Chief Visionary' Discusses His Creation," *New York Times*, 31 January 2002, http://www.nytimes.com, accessed 31 January 2002.

32 Kirsten Lundberg, "Convener or Player? The World Economic Forum and Davos," *Kennedy School of Government Case programme* C15-04-1741.0 (Cambridge MA: Harvard University, 2004): 26.

33 Background interview material provided by World Economic Forum staff, October 2005.

34 Lundberg, "Convener or Player? The World Economic Forum and Davos," 24.

35 *Ibid.*: 26.

36 *Ibid.*: 27.

37 Interview with Ernesto Seman, Argentine diplomat and former journalist, New York, November 2005.

7 The Forum looking ahead

1 The comments that follow are taken from World Economic Forum 2005, Klaus Schwab internal newsletter to World Economic Forum staff, autumn 2005.

2 World Economic Forum 2005, "Roadmap 2008," strategy paper, Cologny, 3 November 2005.

3 World Economic Forum 2005, "Roadmap 2008," 2.

4 The discussion that follows is taken from World Economic Forum 2005, Klaus Schwab address to panel discussion, "Global Challenges and India," at World Economic Forum 2005 India Economic Summit, New Delhi, India, 28 November 2005.

5 Interview with Klaus Schwab, Cologny, Switzerland, May 2005.

6 World Economic Forum 2006, Global Leadership Fellows, http://www.weforum.com, accessed 27 January 2006.

7 Forbes Conferences 2006, http://www.forbesconferences.com, accessed 30 January 2006.

8 Clinton Global Initiative 2006, http://www.clintonglobalinitiative.org, accessed 30 January 2006; John H. Harris, "Bill Clinton Takes Spot on Global Stage," *Washington Post*, 1 June 2005, p. A1, http://www.washingtonpost.com, accessed 5 June 2005.

Select bibliography

Relatively little scholarly research about the World Economic Forum has been published to date. The most useful publications available to help the reader understand what the Forum is achieving are published by the Forum itself. The annual *Global Competitiveness Report* (earlier editions Oxford University Press, later editions Palgrave Macmillan) explains the methodology of the Forum's Global Competitiveness Initiative and contains a series of current substantive scholarly articles addressing issues related to competitiveness. The Forum's other annual publications, such as the *Global Information Technology Report*, provide similar content.

The Forum's Corporate Governance Initiative produced an outstanding volume edited by Peter K. Cornelius and Bruce Kogut, *Corporate Governance and Capital Flows in a Global Economy* (Oxford: Oxford University Press, 2003), which captures the Forum's view of a multi-stakeholder approach to corporate governance.

Of secondary scholarship about the Forum, the closest thing to an institutional history that has appeared thus far is Kirsten Lundberg's paper "Convener or Player? The World Economic Forum and Davos," published by Harvard's Kennedy School of Government for their *Case programme* (Cambridge MA: Harvard University, 2004). Lundberg focuses primarily on management questions, and the timeframe of her research extends up through the late 1990s.

Two articles on the Forum are readily available in scholarly journals. Drawing on French philosopher Georges Sorel's theory of social myth, Jean-Christophe Graz argues in "How Powerful Are Transnational Elite Clubs? The Social Myth of the World Economic Forum' (*New Political Economy* 8, 3, November 2003: 321–40), that as elite organizations such as the World Economic Forum become more democratized and participatory, they become less able to institutionalize the views and perspectives of their memberships amongst the general public.

The second article, "A Multifunctional Case Study for Teaching International Political Economy: The World Economic Forum as Shar-pei or Wolf in Sheep's Clothing?" (*International Studies Perspectives* 3, August 2002: 291–309) prefigures this book in certain respects. In it I examine how different social groups have generated different narratives of the evolution of the Forum, and how the Forum's own narrative of its accomplishments was so successful in the 1990s that it contributed to attracting the attention of critics with different objectives for globalization.

Index

CPSIA information can be obtained
at www.ICGtesting.com
Printed in the USA
LVHW091111040321
680581LV00002B/5